Take It to Your Seat Centers

Math

K

Using the Centers

The 12 centers in this book provide hands-on practice to help students master standards-based mathematics skills. It is important to teach each skill and to model the use of each center before asking students to do the tasks independently. The centers are self-contained and portable. Students can work at a desk, at a table, or on a rug, and they can use the centers as often as needed.

Why Use Centers?

- Centers are a motivating way for students to practice important skills.

- They provide for differentiated instruction.

- They appeal especially to kinesthetic and visual learners.

- They are ready to use whenever instruction or practice in the target skill is indicated.

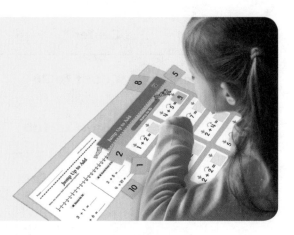

Before Using Centers

You and your students will enjoy using centers more if you think through logistical considerations. Here are a few questions to resolve ahead of time:

- Will students select a center, or will you assign the centers and use them as a skill assessment tool?

- Will there be a specific block of time for centers, or will the centers be used by students throughout the day as they complete other work?

- Where will you place the centers for easy access by students?

- What procedure will students use when they need help with the center tasks?

- Will students use the answer key to check their own work?

- How will you use the center checklist to track completion of the centers?

Introducing the Centers

Use the teacher instructions page and the student directions on the center's cover page to teach or review the skill. Show students the pieces of the center and model how to use them as you read each step of the directions.

If you find some of the skills too challenging for your students, you may want to use one or more of the centers only for group work, or you might use the center several times with a group before assigning it for independent use. You also have the option of assigning only part of a center for independent work.

Recording Progress

Use the center checklist (page 4) to record both the date when a student completes each center and the student's skill level at that point.

Making the Centers

Included for Each Center

(A) Student directions/cover page

(B) Task cards and/or mat(s)

(C) Reproducible written practice

(D) Answer key

Materials Needed

- Folders with inside pockets

- Small envelopes or self-closing plastic bags (for storing task cards)

- Pencils or marking pens (for labeling envelopes)

- Scissors

- Double-sided tape (for attaching the cover page to the front of the folder)

- Laminating equipment

How to Assemble and Store

1. Tape the center's cover page to the front of the folder.

2. Place reproduced written practice pages in the left-hand pocket of the folder.

3. Laminate mats and task cards.

4. Cut apart the task cards and put them in a labeled envelope or self-closing plastic bag. Place the mats and task cards in the right-hand pocket of the folder. If you want the centers to be self-checking, include the answer key in the folder.

5. Store prepared centers in a file box or a crate.

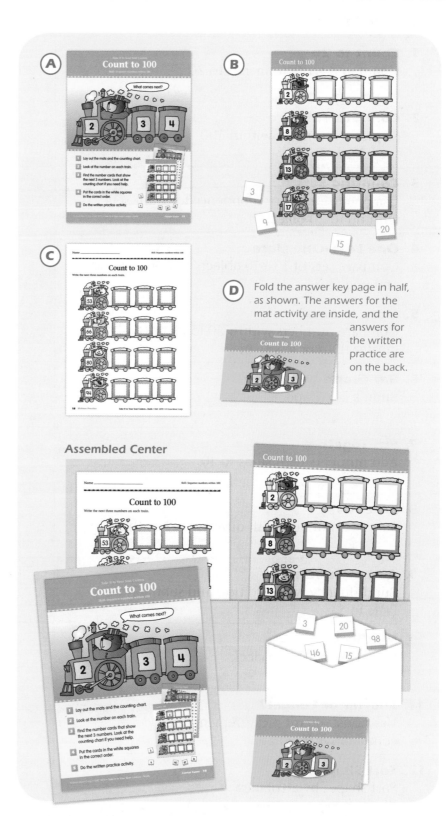

(D) Fold the answer key page in half, as shown. The answers for the mat activity are inside, and the answers for the written practice are on the back.

Assembled Center

Student _____

Center Checklist

Center / Skill	Skill Level	Date
1. Count to 20 Count and write numerals to 20		
2. Count to 100 Sequence numbers within 100		
3. Counting Sets Use one-to-one correspondence to count sets with up to 20 objects		
4. One Less–One More Compare sets of 1 to 10 objects to find one less and one more		
5. More or Less? Compare numbers within 20 to identify greater than or less than		
6. Bar Graph Build a bar graph		
7. Put Together Add numbers with sums to 10		
8. Take Away Subtract numbers with differences less than 10		
9. Add or Subtract Build fluency with addition and subtraction facts to 5		
10. My Clock Know the parts of a clock		
11. Shorter or Longer? Use nonstandard measurement and comparative language		
12. Sort Shapes Sort shapes by attributes		

Take It to Your Seat Centers—Math • EMC 3070 • © Evan-Moor Corp.

Count to 20

Written Practice

Card Envelope

Center Cover

Answer Key

Cards

Skill: Count and write numerals to 20

Steps to Follow

1. **Prepare the center.** (See page 3.)

2. **Introduce the center.** State the goal. Say: *You will put the caterpillar parts in number order to count from 1 to 20.*

3. **Teach the skill.** Demonstrate how to use the center with individual students or small groups.

4. **Practice the skill.** Have students use the center independently or with a partner.

Contents

Count to 20

Write the missing numbers to count to **20**.

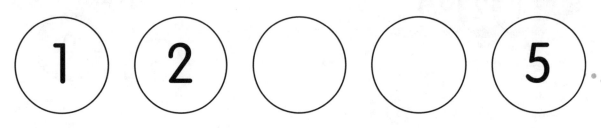

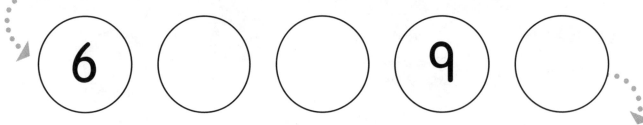

Count to 20

Skill: Count and write numerals to 20

1. Lay out the caterpillar parts.

2. Put the parts in number order to make the whole caterpillar. Begin with **1**.

3. Then point to each number on the caterpillar and count.

4. Do the written practice activity.

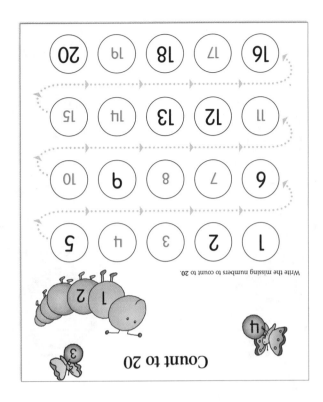

Write the missing numbers to count to 20.

Count to 20

Written Practice

(fold)

Answer Key

Count to 20

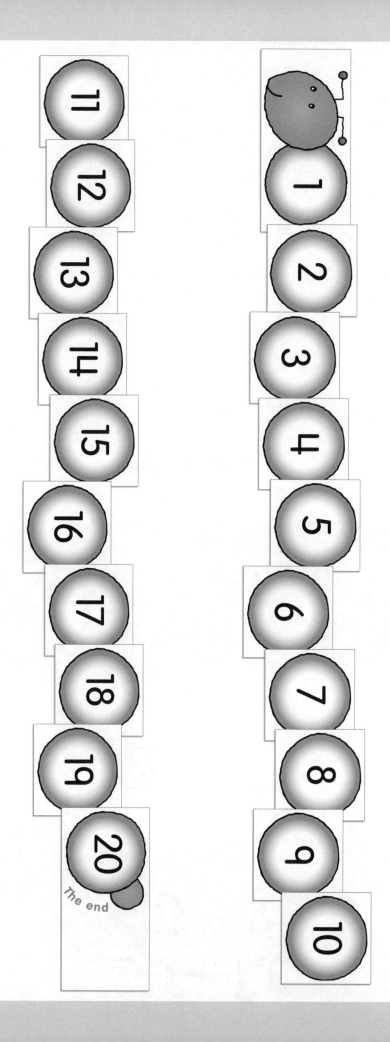

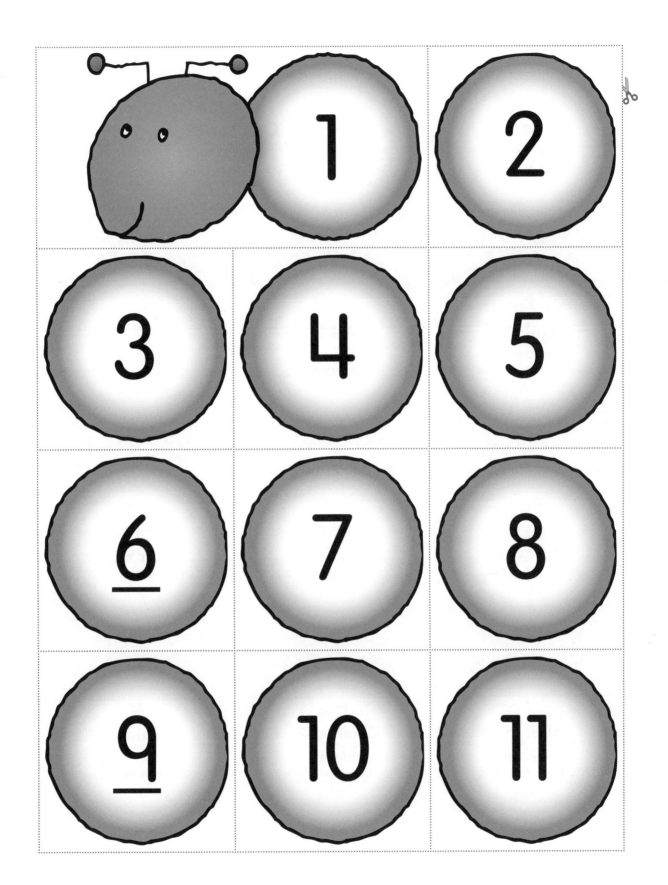

Count to 20

EMC 3070
© Evan-Moor Corp.

Count to 20

EMC 3070
© Evan-Moor Corp.

Count to 20

EMC 3070
© Evan-Moor Corp.

Count to 20

EMC 3070
© Evan-Moor Corp.

Count to 20

EMC 3070
© Evan-Moor Corp.

Count to 20

EMC 3070
© Evan-Moor Corp.

Count to 20

EMC 3070
© Evan-Moor Corp.

Count to 20

EMC 3070
© Evan-Moor Corp.

Count to 20

EMC 3070
© Evan-Moor Corp.

Count to 20

EMC 3070
© Evan-Moor Corp.

Count to 20

EMC 3070
© Evan-Moor Corp.

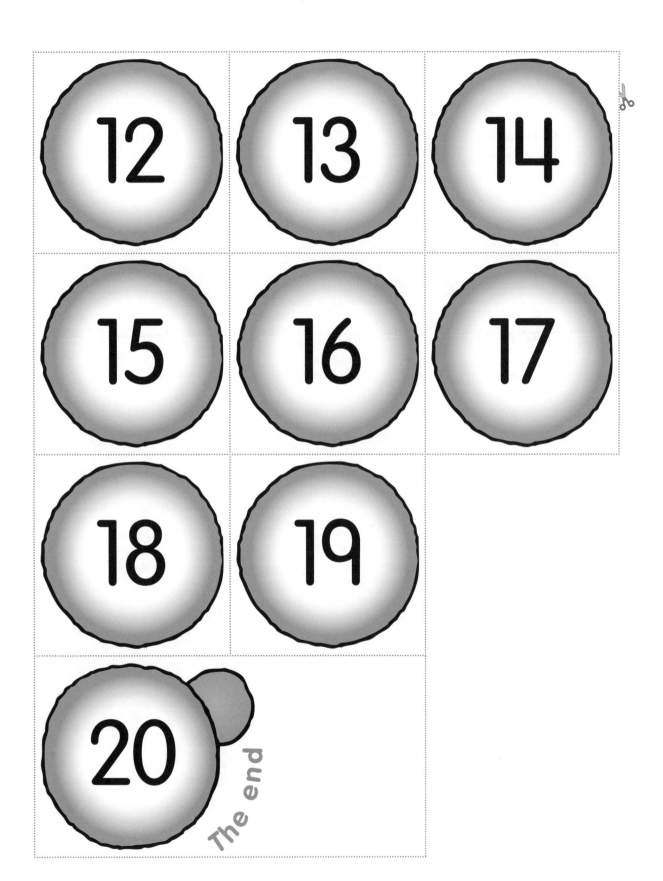

The end

Count to 20

EMC 3070
© Evan-Moor Corp.

Count to 20

EMC 3070
© Evan-Moor Corp.

Count to 20

EMC 3070
© Evan-Moor Corp.

Count to 20

EMC 3070
© Evan-Moor Corp.

Count to 20

EMC 3070
© Evan-Moor Corp.

Count to 20

EMC 3070
© Evan-Moor Corp.

Count to 20

EMC 3070
© Evan-Moor Corp.

Count to 20

EMC 3070
© Evan-Moor Corp.

Count to 20

EMC 3070
© Evan-Moor Corp.

Caterpillar Pocket

(See instructions on page 16.)

Count to 20

How to Make the Caterpillar Pocket

1. Cut along the dotted lines.
2. Fold the bottom part up.
3. Staple or tape the sides to form the pocket.
4. Fold the top part down.
5. Put the caterpillar parts inside.

top *(fold down)*

bottom *(fold up)*

Take It to Your Seat Centers—Math • EMC 3070 • © Evan-Moor Corp.

Count to 100

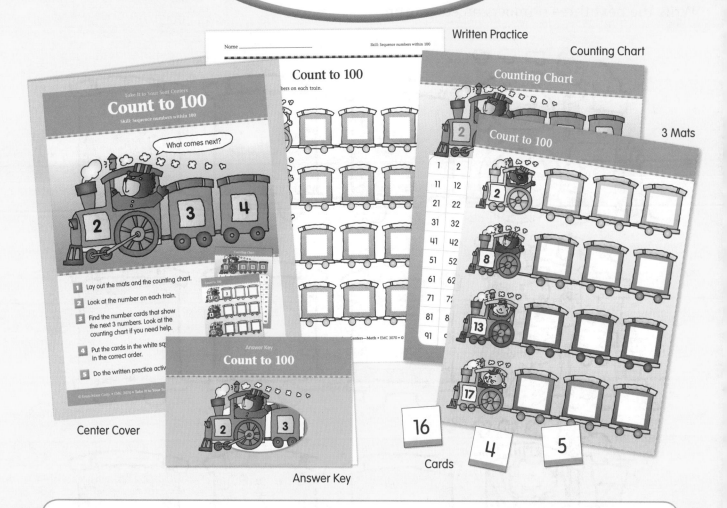

Written Practice

Counting Chart

3 Mats

Center Cover

Answer Key

Cards

Skill: Sequence numbers within 100

Steps to Follow

1. **Prepare the center.** (See page 3.)

2. **Introduce the center.** State the goal. Say: *You will place cards in each row on the mats to show the numbers that come next. You may look at the counting chart for help.*

3. **Teach the skill.** Demonstrate how to use the center with individual students or small groups.

4. **Practice the skill.** Have students use the center independently or with a partner.

Contents

Count to 100

Write the next three numbers on each train.

Take It to Your Seat Centers—Math • EMC 3070 • © Evan-Moor Corp.

Count to 100

Skill: Sequence numbers within 100

1   Lay out the mats and the counting chart.

2   Look at the number on each train.

3   Find the number cards that show the next 3 numbers. Look at the counting chart if you need help.

4   Put the cards in the white squares in the correct order.

5   Do the written practice activity.

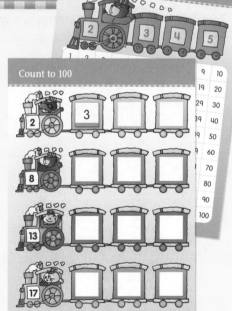

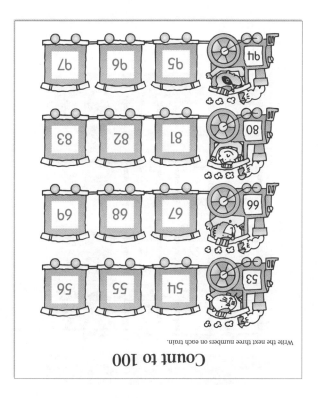

Write the next three numbers on each train.

Count to 100

Written Practice

(fold)

Answer Key

Count to 100

Count to 100

Count to 100

58	59	60	61
70	71	72	73
86	87	88	89
97	98	99	100

Counting Chart

1	2	3	4	5	6	7	8	9	10
11	12	13	14	15	16	17	18	19	20
21	22	23	24	25	26	27	28	29	30
31	32	33	34	35	36	37	38	39	40
41	42	43	44	45	46	47	48	49	50
51	52	53	54	55	56	57	58	59	60
61	62	63	64	65	66	67	68	69	70
71	72	73	74	75	76	77	78	79	80
81	82	83	84	85	86	87	88	89	90
91	92	93	94	95	96	97	98	99	100

Take It to Your Seat Centers—Math • EMC 3070 • © Evan-Moor Corp.

Count to 100

Count to 100

3	4	5	9	10	11
14	15	16	18	19	20
25	26	27	32	33	34
40	41	42	46	47	48
59	60	61	71	72	73
87	88	89	98	99	100

Count to 100

EMC 3070

© Evan-Moor Corp.

Count to 100

EMC 3070

© Evan-Moor Corp.

Count to 100

EMC 3070

© Evan-Moor Corp.

Count to 100

EMC 3070

© Evan-Moor Corp.

Count to 100

EMC 3070

© Evan-Moor Corp.

Count to 100

EMC 3070

© Evan-Moor Corp.

Count to 100

EMC 3070

© Evan-Moor Corp.

Count to 100

EMC 3070

© Evan-Moor Corp.

Count to 100

EMC 3070

© Evan-Moor Corp.

Count to 100

EMC 3070

© Evan-Moor Corp.

Count to 100

EMC 3070

© Evan-Moor Corp.

Count to 100

EMC 3070

© Evan-Moor Corp.

Count to 100

EMC 3070

© Evan-Moor Corp.

Count to 100

EMC 3070

© Evan-Moor Corp.

Count to 100

EMC 3070

© Evan-Moor Corp.

Count to 100

EMC 3070

© Evan-Moor Corp.

Count to 100

EMC 3070

© Evan-Moor Corp.

Count to 100

EMC 3070

© Evan-Moor Corp.

Count to 100

EMC 3070

© Evan-Moor Corp.

Count to 100

EMC 3070

© Evan-Moor Corp.

Count to 100

EMC 3070

© Evan-Moor Corp.

Count to 100

EMC 3070

© Evan-Moor Corp.

Count to 100

EMC 3070

© Evan-Moor Corp.

Count to 100

EMC 3070

© Evan-Moor Corp.

Count to 100

EMC 3070

© Evan-Moor Corp.

Count to 100

EMC 3070

© Evan-Moor Corp.

Count to 100

EMC 3070

© Evan-Moor Corp.

Count to 100

EMC 3070

© Evan-Moor Corp.

Count to 100

EMC 3070

© Evan-Moor Corp.

Count to 100

EMC 3070

© Evan-Moor Corp.

Count to 100

EMC 3070

© Evan-Moor Corp.

Count to 100

EMC 3070

© Evan-Moor Corp.

Count to 100

EMC 3070

© Evan-Moor Corp.

Count to 100

EMC 3070

© Evan-Moor Corp.

Count to 100

EMC 3070

© Evan-Moor Corp.

Count to 100

EMC 3070

© Evan-Moor Corp.

Counting Sets

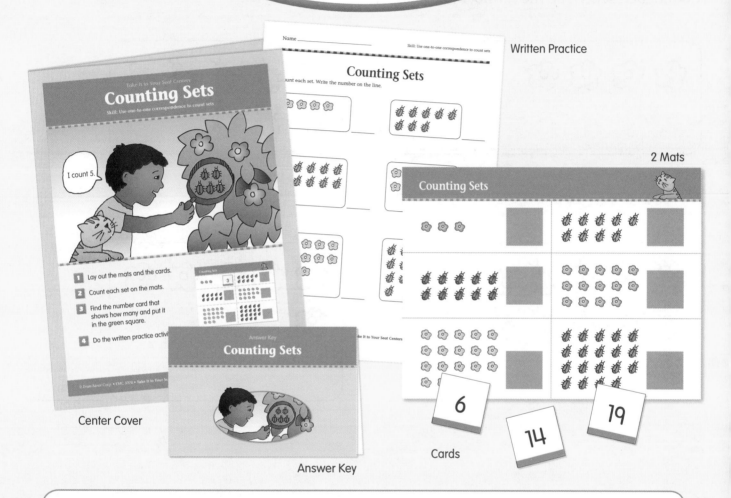

Written Practice

2 Mats

Cards

Center Cover

Answer Key

Skill: Use one-to-one correspondence to count sets with up to 20 objects

Steps to Follow

1. **Prepare the center.** (See page 3.)

2. **Introduce the center.** State the goal. Say: *You will count each set of objects on the mats and find the correct number card.*

3. **Teach the skill.** Demonstrate how to use the center with individual students or small groups.

4. **Practice the skill.** Have students use the center independently or with a partner.

Contents

Counting Sets

Count each set. Write the number on the line.

_____

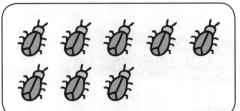

_____

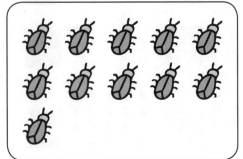

_____

_____

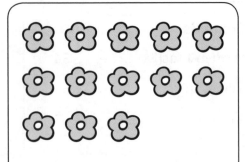

_____

_____

Counting Sets

Skill: Use one-to-one correspondence to count sets

1. Lay out the mats and the cards.

2. Count each set on the mats.

3. Find the number card that shows how many and put it in the green square.

4. Do the written practice activity.

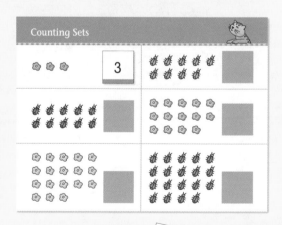

Counting Sets

Count each set. Write the number on the line.

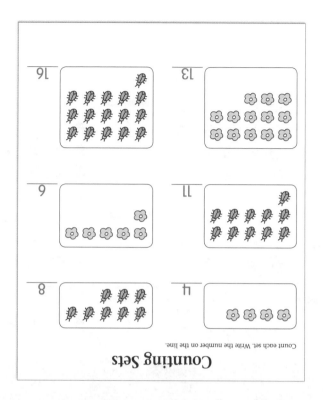

16

13

9

11

8

4

(fold)

Answer Key

Counting Sets

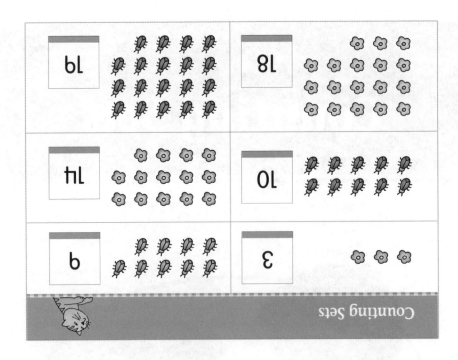

Counting Sets

19	18
14	10
9	3

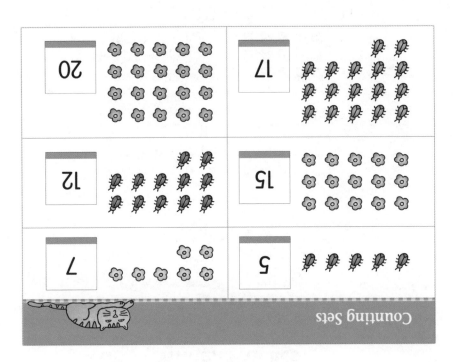

Counting Sets

20	17
12	15
7	5

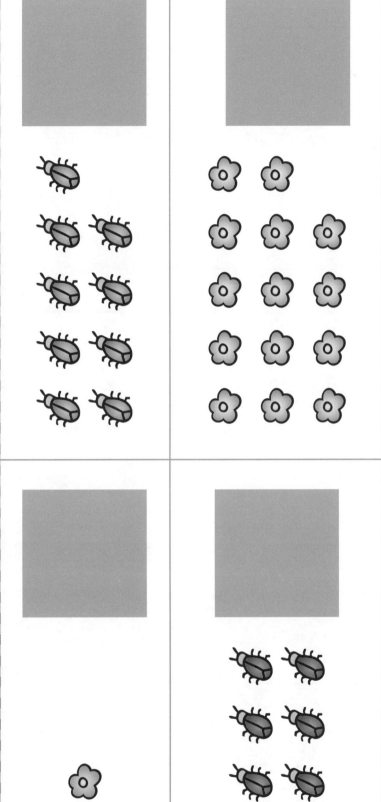

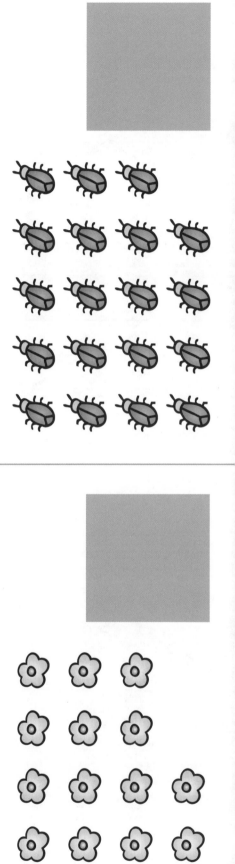

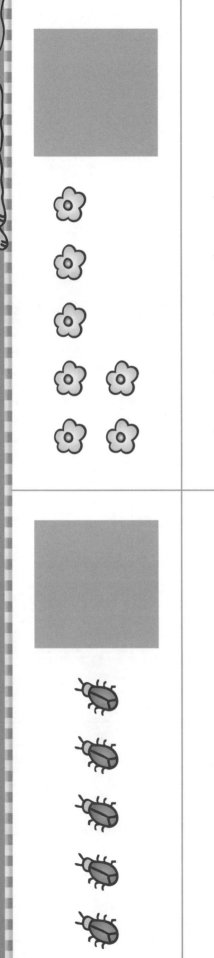

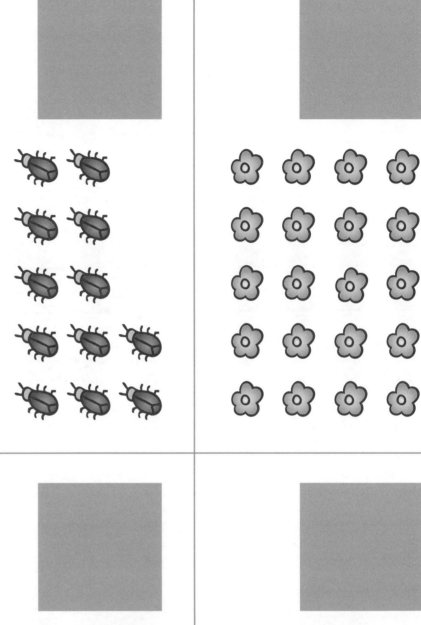

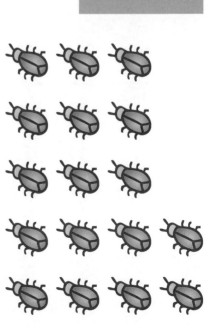

1	2	3	4
5	9	7	8
9	10	11	12
13	14	15	16
17	18	19	20

Counting Sets
EMC 3070
© Evan-Moor Corp.

Counting Sets
EMC 3070
© Evan-Moor Corp.

Counting Sets
EMC 3070
© Evan-Moor Corp.

Counting Sets
EMC 3070
© Evan-Moor Corp.

Counting Sets
EMC 3070
© Evan-Moor Corp.

Counting Sets
EMC 3070
© Evan-Moor Corp.

Counting Sets
EMC 3070
© Evan-Moor Corp.

Counting Sets
EMC 3070
© Evan-Moor Corp.

Counting Sets
EMC 3070
© Evan-Moor Corp.

Counting Sets
EMC 3070
© Evan-Moor Corp.

Counting Sets
EMC 3070
© Evan-Moor Corp.

Counting Sets
EMC 3070
© Evan-Moor Corp.

Counting Sets
EMC 3070
© Evan-Moor Corp.

Counting Sets
EMC 3070
© Evan-Moor Corp.

Counting Sets
EMC 3070
© Evan-Moor Corp.

Counting Sets
EMC 3070
© Evan-Moor Corp.

One Less One More

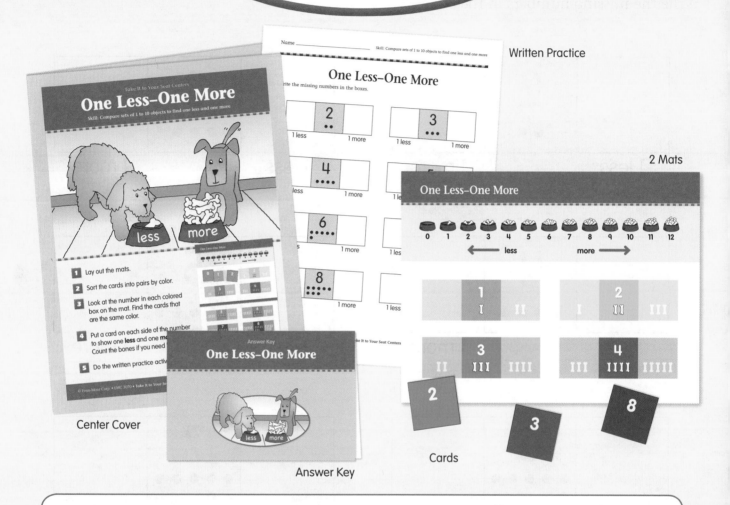

Written Practice

2 Mats

Center Cover

Answer Key

Cards

Skill: Compare sets of 1 to 10 objects to find one less and one more

Steps to Follow

1. **Prepare the center.** (See page 3.)

2. **Introduce the center.** State the goal. Say:
   You will place number cards on both sides of each number on the mats to show one less and one more.

3. **Teach the skill.** Demonstrate how to use the center with individual students or small groups.

4. **Practice the skill.** Have students use the center independently or with a partner.

Contents

One Less–One More

Write the missing numbers in the boxes.

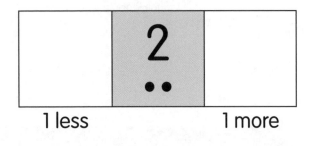

1 less   1 more

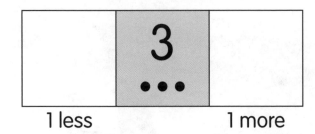

1 less   1 more

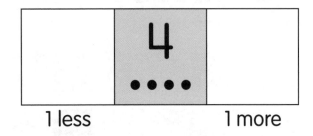

1 less   1 more

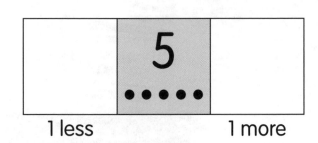

1 less   1 more

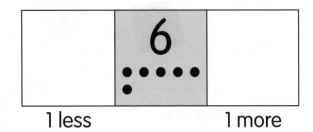

1 less   1 more

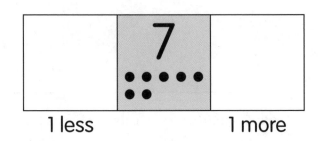

1 less   1 more

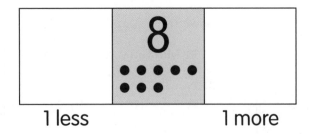

1 less   1 more

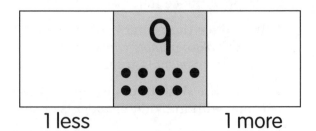

1 less   1 more

One Less–One More

Skill: Compare sets of 1 to 10 objects to find one less and one more

1. Lay out the mats.

2. Sort the cards into pairs by color.

3. Look at the number in each colored box on the mat. Find the cards that are the same color.

4. Put a card on each side of the number to show one **less** and one **more**. Count the bones if you need help.

5. Do the written practice activity.

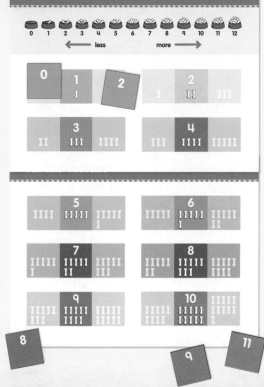

One Less–One More

Write the missing numbers in the boxes.

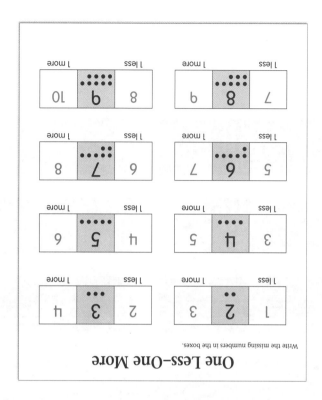

1 less		1 more
8	9	10
6	7	8
4	5	6
2	3	4
7	8	9
5	6	7
3	4	5
1	2	3

(fold)

Answer Key

One Less–One More

less   more

One Less–One More

One Less–One More

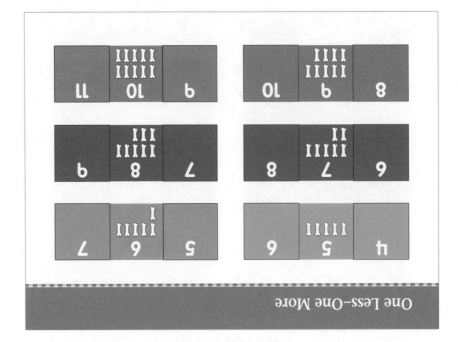

One Less–One More

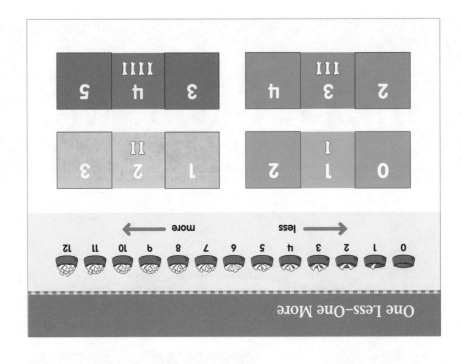

One Less—One More

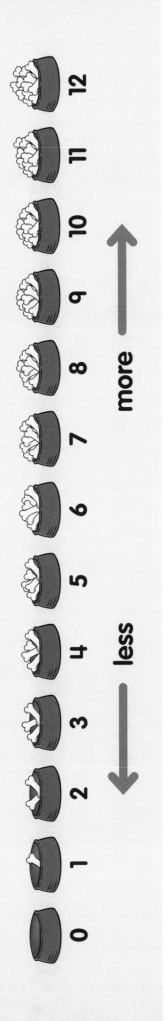

0 1 2 3 4 5 6 7 8 9 10 11 12

← less   more →

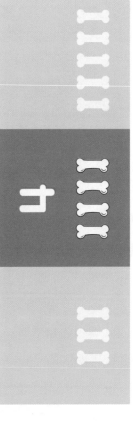

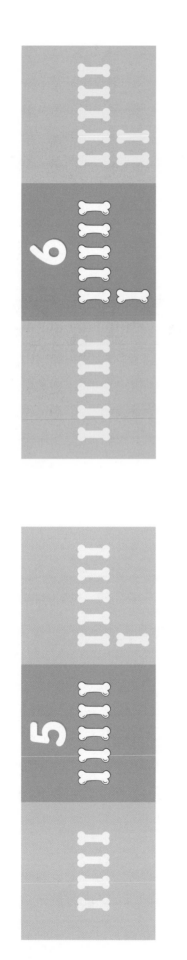

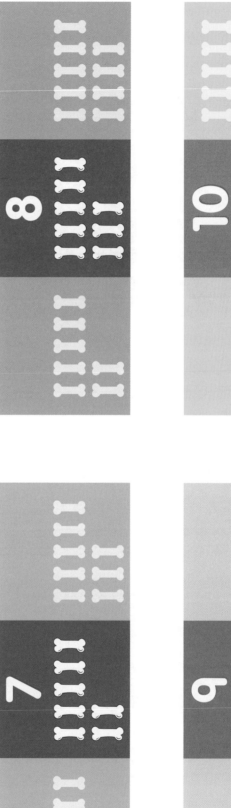

5	7		7	9
6	8		3	5
4	6		0	2
9	11		1	3
8	10		2	4

One Less–One More	One Less–One More	One Less–One More	One Less–One More
EMC 3070	EMC 3070	EMC 3070	EMC 3070
© Evan-Moor Corp.	© Evan-Moor Corp.	© Evan-Moor Corp.	© Evan-Moor Corp.
One Less–One More	One Less–One More	One Less–One More	One Less–One More
EMC 3070	EMC 3070	EMC 3070	EMC 3070
© Evan-Moor Corp.	© Evan-Moor Corp.	© Evan-Moor Corp.	© Evan-Moor Corp.
One Less–One More	One Less–One More	One Less–One More	One Less–One More
EMC 3070	EMC 3070	EMC 3070	EMC 3070
© Evan-Moor Corp.	© Evan-Moor Corp.	© Evan-Moor Corp.	© Evan-Moor Corp.
One Less–One More	One Less–One More	One Less–One More	One Less–One More
EMC 3070	EMC 3070	EMC 3070	EMC 3070
© Evan-Moor Corp.	© Evan-Moor Corp.	© Evan-Moor Corp.	© Evan-Moor Corp.
One Less–One More	One Less–One More	One Less–One More	One Less–One More
EMC 3070	EMC 3070	EMC 3070	EMC 3070
© Evan-Moor Corp.	© Evan-Moor Corp.	© Evan-Moor Corp.	© Evan-Moor Corp.

More or Less?

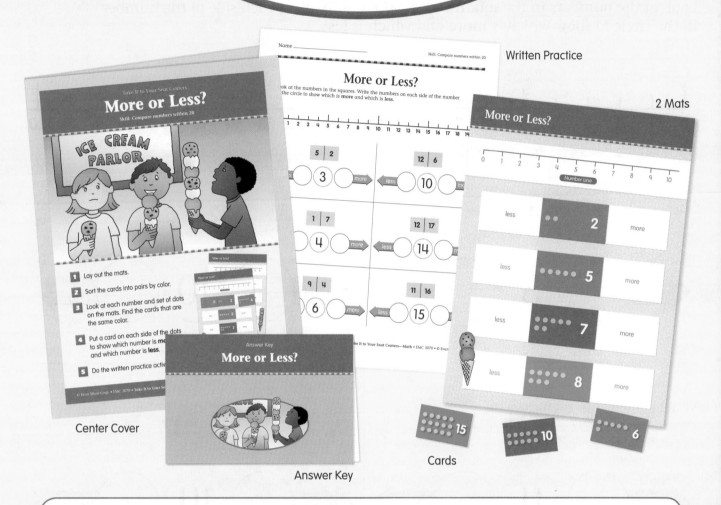

Written Practice

2 Mats

Center Cover

Answer Key

Cards

Skill: Compare numbers within 20 to identify greater than or less than

Steps to Follow

1. **Prepare the center.** (See page 3.)

2. **Introduce the center.** State the goal. Say: *You will place matching colored cards next to each number on the mats to show which number is more and which number is less.*

3. **Teach the skill.** Demonstrate how to use the center with individual students or small groups.

4. **Practice the skill.** Have students use the center independently or with a partner.

Contents

More or Less?

Look at the numbers in the squares. Write the numbers on each side of the number in the circle to show which is **more** and which is **less**.

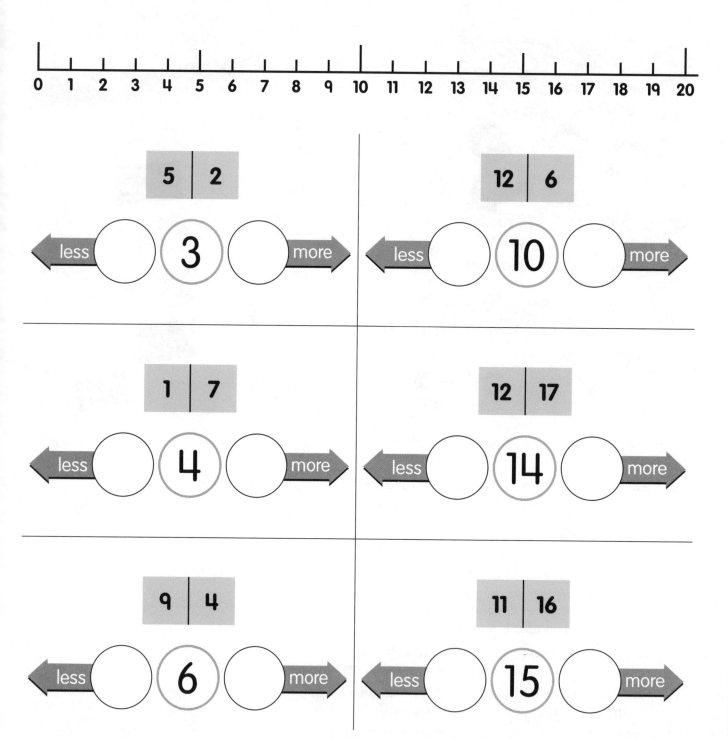

More or Less?

Skill: Compare numbers within 20

1. Lay out the mats.

2. Sort the cards into pairs by color.

3. Look at each number and set of dots on the mats. Find the cards that are the same color.

4. Put a card on each side of the dots to show which number is **more** and which number is **less**.

5. Do the written practice activity.

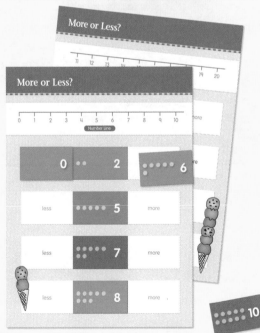

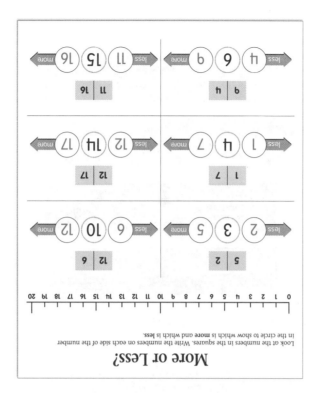

More or Less?

Look at the numbers in the squares. Write the numbers on each side of the number in the circle to show which is **more** and which is **less**.

Written Practice

(fold)

More or Less?

Answer Key

More or Less?

More or Less?

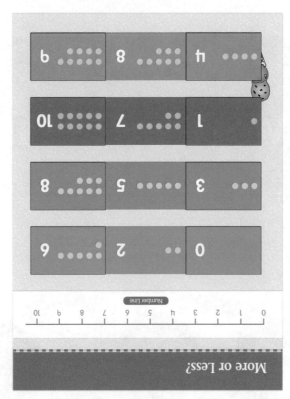

More or Less?

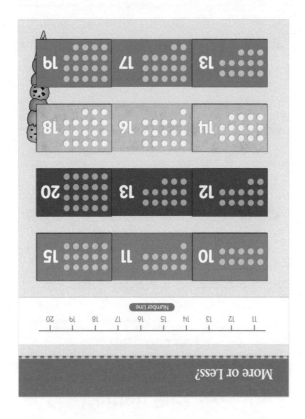

More or Less?

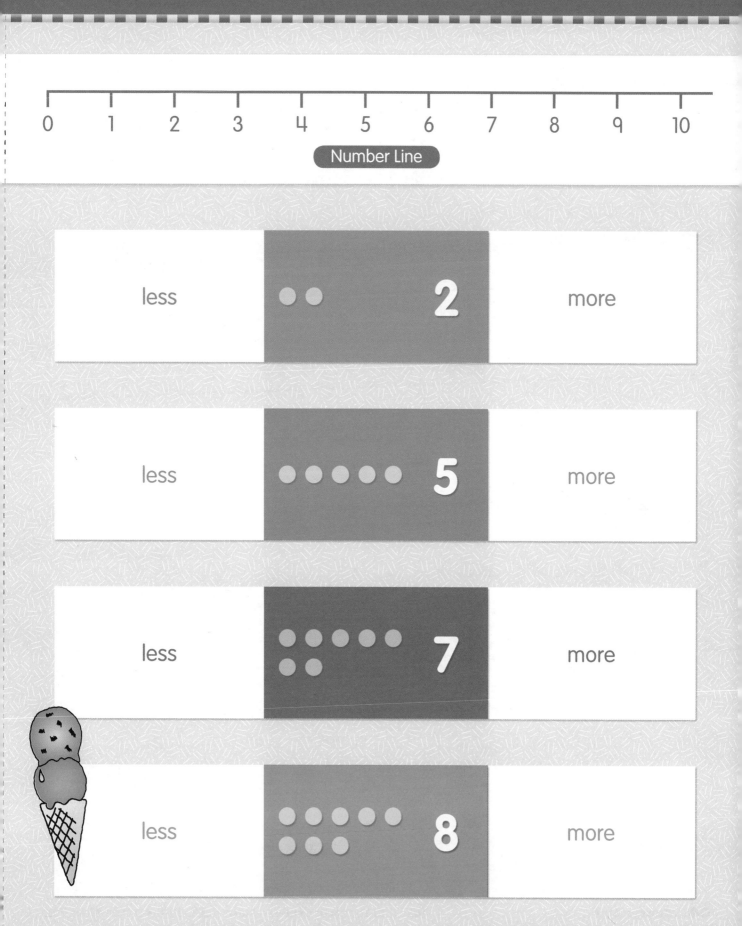

	Number Line	
0 1 2 3 4 5 6 7 8 9 10		

less	●● **2**	more
less	●●●●● **5**	more
less	●●●●● ●● **7**	more
less	●●●●● ●●● **8**	more

More or Less?

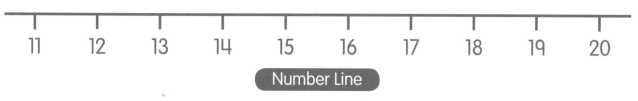

11 12 13 14 15 16 17 18 19 20

Number Line

| less | 11 | more |

| less | 13 | more |

| less | 16 | more |

| less | 17 | more |

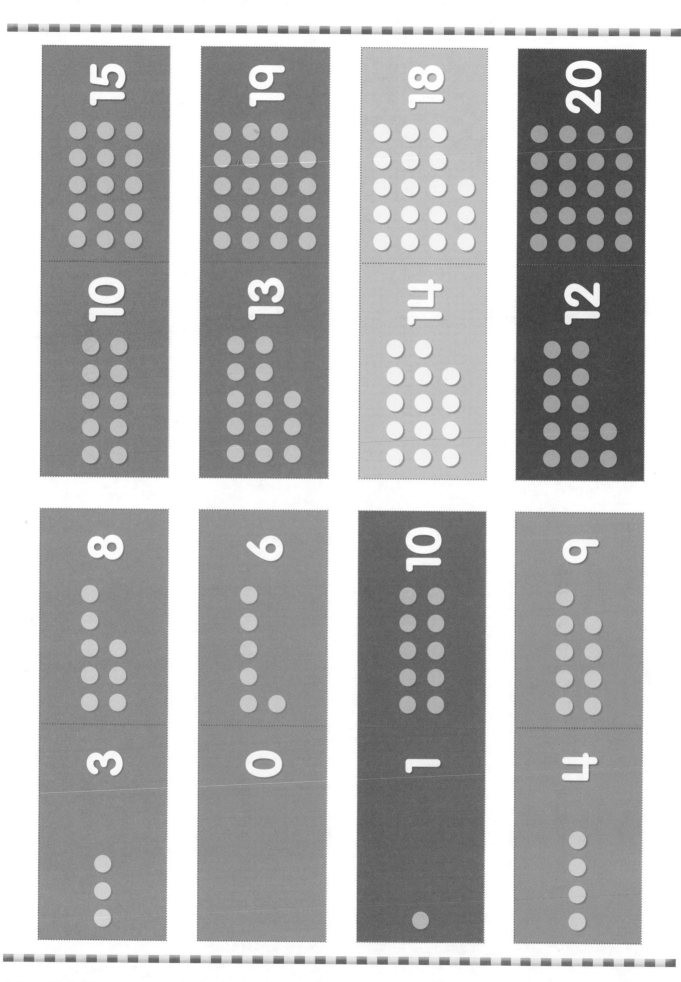

More or Less?

EMC 3070
© Evan-Moor Corp.

More or Less?

EMC 3070
© Evan-Moor Corp.

More or Less?

EMC 3070
© Evan-Moor Corp.

More or Less?

EMC 3070
© Evan-Moor Corp.

More or Less?

EMC 3070
© Evan-Moor Corp.

More or Less?

EMC 3070
© Evan-Moor Corp.

More or Less?

EMC 3070
© Evan-Moor Corp.

More or Less?

EMC 3070
© Evan-Moor Corp.

More or Less?

EMC 3070
© Evan-Moor Corp.

More or Less?

EMC 3070
© Evan-Moor Corp.

More or Less?

EMC 3070
© Evan-Moor Corp.

More or Less?

EMC 3070
© Evan-Moor Corp.

Bar Graph

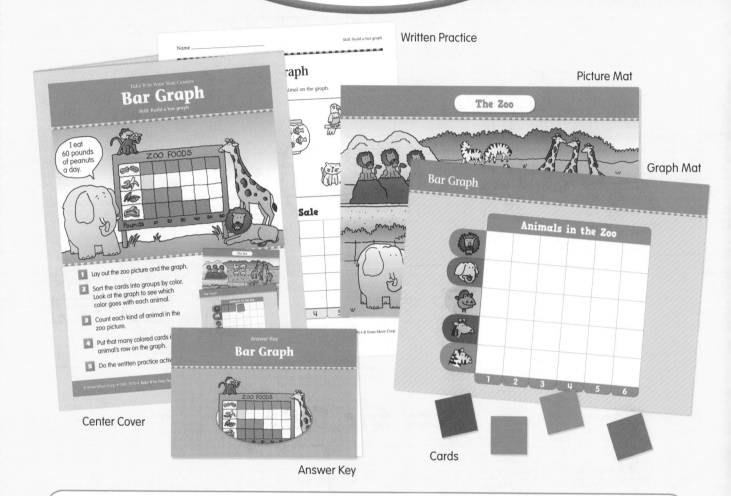

Written Practice

Picture Mat

Graph Mat

Center Cover

Answer Key

Cards

Skill: Build a bar graph

Steps to Follow

1. **Prepare the center.** (See page 3.)

2. **Introduce the center.** State the goal. Say: *You will count animals and make a bar graph to show how many of each kind of animal you counted.*

3. **Teach the skill.** Demonstrate how to use the center with individual students or small groups.

4. **Practice the skill.** Have students use the center independently or with a partner.

Contents

Bar Graph

Count the number of animals in each group.
Color the same number of squares next to that animal on the graph.

Pets for Sale

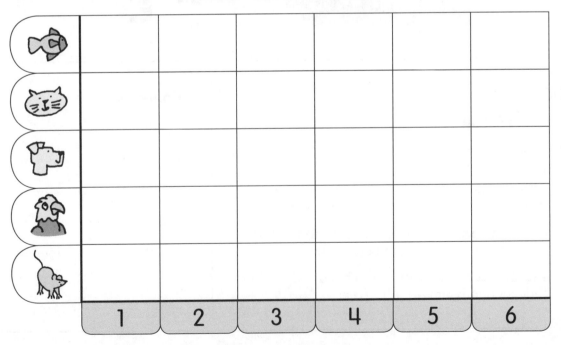

Bar Graph

Skill: Build a bar graph

1. Lay out the zoo picture and the graph.

2. Sort the cards into groups by color. Look at the graph to see which color goes with each animal.

3. Count each kind of animal in the zoo picture.

4. Put that many colored cards in the animal's row on the graph.

5. Do the written practice activity.

Bar Graph

Count the number of animals in each group.
Color the same number of squares next to that animal on the graph.

Pets for Sale

Written Practice

(fold)

Answer Key

Bar Graph

Bar Graph

Bar Graph

Animals in the Zoo

The Zoo

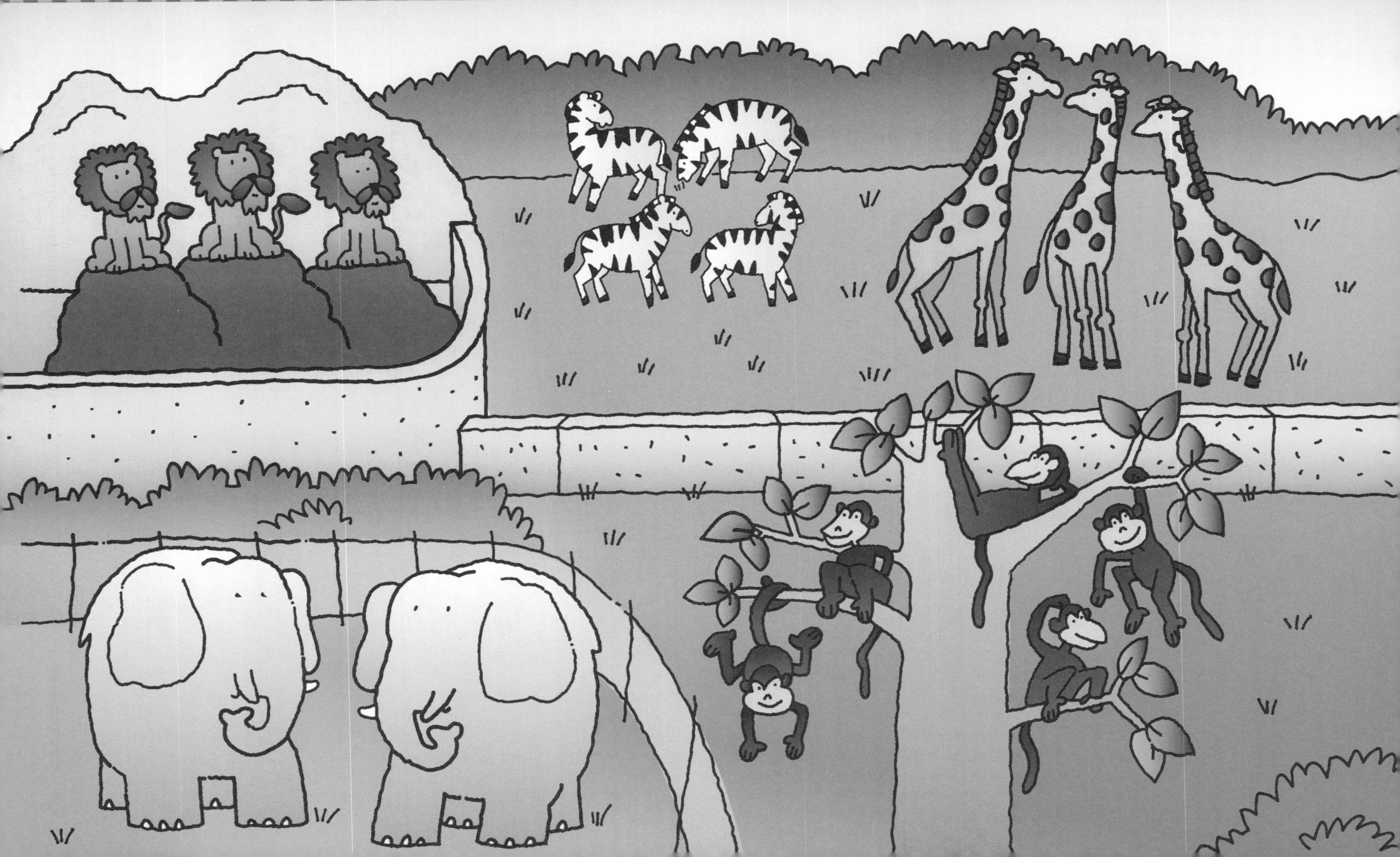

Bar Graph

Animals in the Zoo

	1	2	3	4	5	6

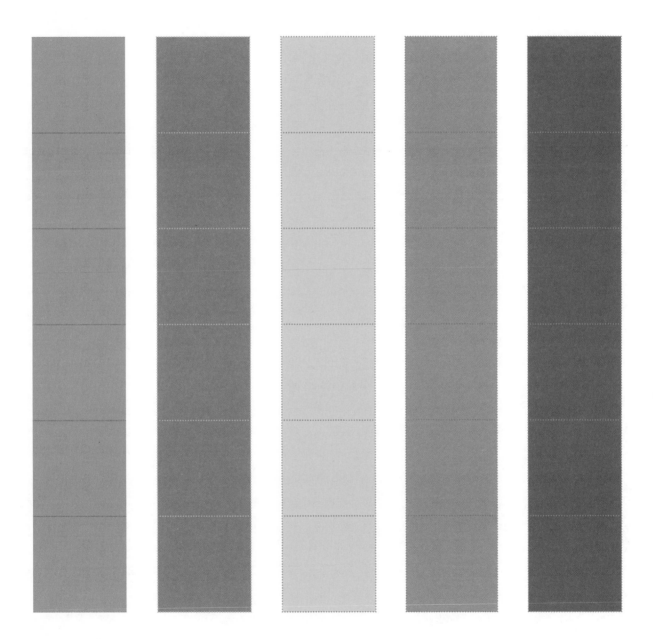

Bar Graph
EMC 3070
© Evan-Moor Corp.

Bar Graph
EMC 3070
© Evan-Moor Corp.

Bar Graph
EMC 3070
© Evan-Moor Corp.

Bar Graph
EMC 3070
© Evan-Moor Corp.

Bar Graph
EMC 3070
© Evan-Moor Corp.

Bar Graph
EMC 3070
© Evan-Moor Corp.

Bar Graph
EMC 3070
© Evan-Moor Corp.

Bar Graph
EMC 3070
© Evan-Moor Corp.

Bar Graph
EMC 3070
© Evan-Moor Corp.

Bar Graph
EMC 3070
© Evan-Moor Corp.

Bar Graph
EMC 3070
© Evan-Moor Corp.

Bar Graph
EMC 3070
© Evan-Moor Corp.

Bar Graph
EMC 3070
© Evan-Moor Corp.

Bar Graph
EMC 3070
© Evan-Moor Corp.

Bar Graph
EMC 3070
© Evan-Moor Corp.

Bar Graph
EMC 3070
© Evan-Moor Corp.

Bar Graph
EMC 3070
© Evan-Moor Corp.

Bar Graph
EMC 3070
© Evan-Moor Corp.

Bar Graph
EMC 3070
© Evan-Moor Corp.

Bar Graph
EMC 3070
© Evan-Moor Corp.

Bar Graph
EMC 3070
© Evan-Moor Corp.

Bar Graph
EMC 3070
© Evan-Moor Corp.

Bar Graph
EMC 3070
© Evan-Moor Corp.

Bar Graph
EMC 3070
© Evan-Moor Corp.

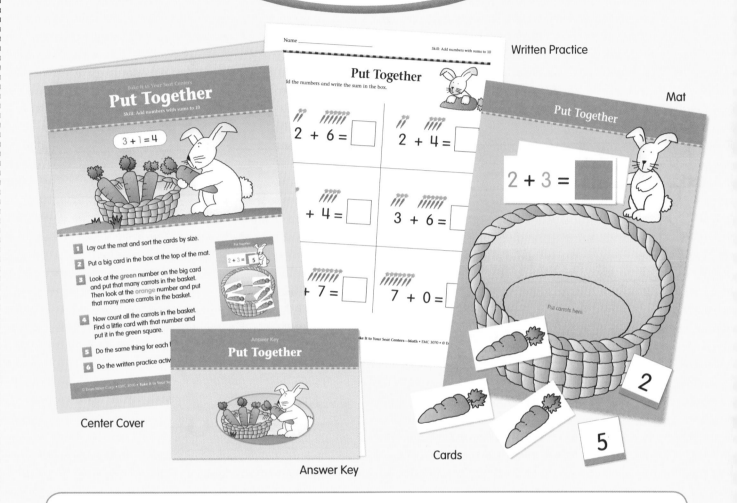

Take It to Your Seat Centers

Put Together

Written Practice

Mat

Center Cover

Answer Key

Cards

Skill: Add numbers with sums to 10

Steps to Follow

1. **Prepare the center.** (See page 3.)

2. **Introduce the center.** State the goal. Say: *You will count carrots and put them together in a basket to help you add two numbers.*

3. **Teach the skill.** Demonstrate how to use the center with individual students or small groups.

4. **Practice the skill.** Have students use the center independently or with a partner.

Contents

Put Together

Add the numbers and write the sum in the box.

2 + 6 = ☐

2 + 4 = ☐

1 + 4 = ☐

3 + 6 = ☐

3 + 7 = ☐

7 + 0 = ☐

Put Together

Skill: Add numbers with sums to 10

3 + 1 = 4

1 Lay out the mat and sort the cards by size.

2 Put a big card in the box at the top of the mat.

3 Look at the **green** number on the big card and put that many carrots in the basket. Then look at the **orange** number and put that many more carrots in the basket.

4 Now count all the carrots in the basket. Find a little card with that number and put it in the green square.

5 Do the same thing for each big card.

6 Do the written practice activity.

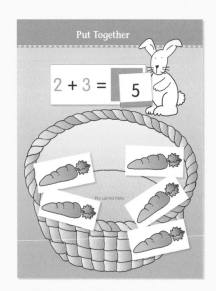

Put Together

2 + 3 = 5

5 + 2 =

Put Together

Add the numbers and write the sum in the box.

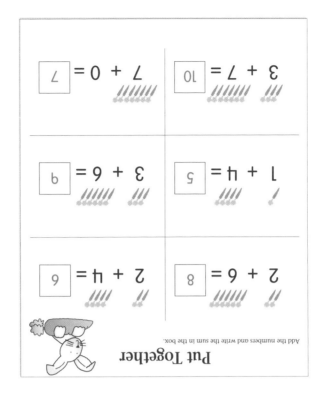

$3 + 7 = \boxed{10}$

$7 + 0 = \boxed{7}$

$3 + 6 = \boxed{9}$

$1 + 4 = \boxed{5}$

$2 + 4 = \boxed{6}$

$2 + 6 = \boxed{8}$

Written Practice

(fold)

Answer Key

Put Together

Put Together

4 + 5 = 9

3 + 4 = 7

2 + 7 = 9

4 + 2 = 6

1 + 5 = 6

6 + 2 = 8

5 + 0 = 5

6 + 4 = 10

5 + 2 = 7

3 + 5 = 8

8 + 2 = 10

2 + 3 = 5

Put Together

Put big card here.

Put carrots here.

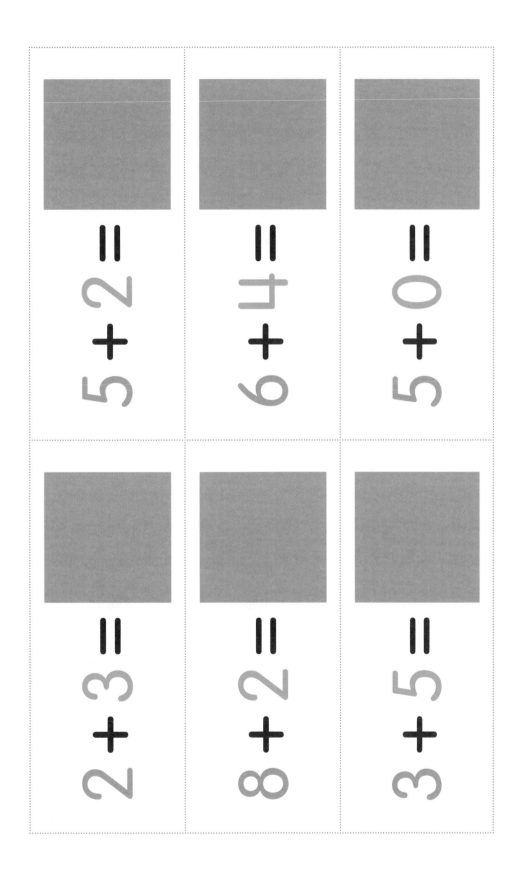

5 + 2 =

6 + 4 =

5 + 0 =

2 + 3 =

8 + 2 =

3 + 5 =

Put Together

EMC 3070

© Evan-Moor Corp.

Put Together

EMC 3070

© Evan-Moor Corp.

Put Together

EMC 3070

© Evan-Moor Corp.

Put Together

EMC 3070

© Evan-Moor Corp.

Put Together

EMC 3070

© Evan-Moor Corp.

Put Together

EMC 3070

© Evan-Moor Corp.

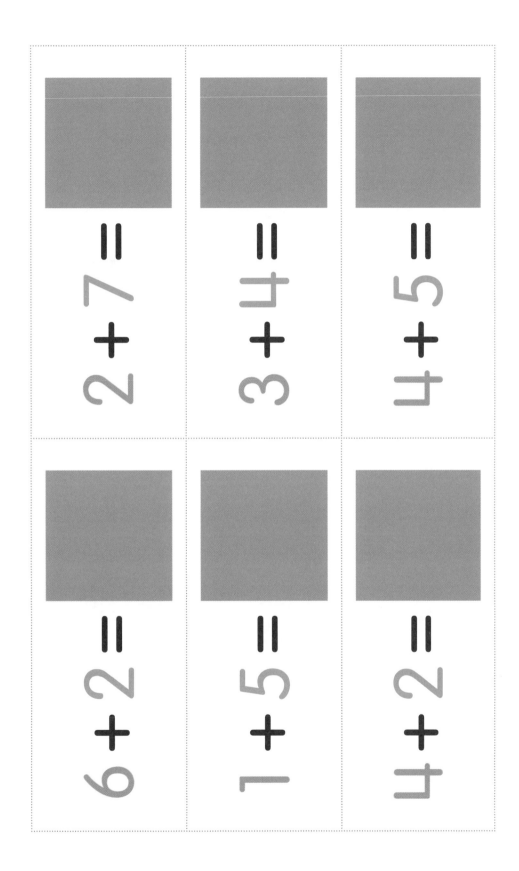

Put Together

EMC 3070

© Evan-Moor Corp.

Put Together

EMC 3070

© Evan-Moor Corp.

Put Together

EMC 3070

© Evan-Moor Corp.

Put Together

EMC 3070

© Evan-Moor Corp.

Put Together

EMC 3070

© Evan-Moor Corp.

Put Together

EMC 3070

© Evan-Moor Corp.

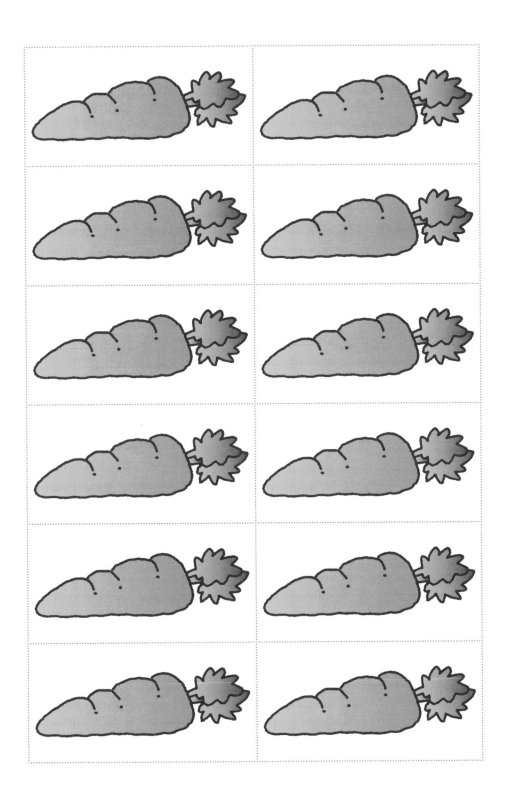

Put Together

EMC 3070
© Evan-Moor Corp.

Put Together

EMC 3070
© Evan-Moor Corp.

Put Together

EMC 3070
© Evan-Moor Corp.

Put Together

EMC 3070
© Evan-Moor Corp.

Put Together

EMC 3070
© Evan-Moor Corp.

Put Together

EMC 3070
© Evan-Moor Corp.

Put Together

EMC 3070
© Evan-Moor Corp.

Put Together

EMC 3070
© Evan-Moor Corp.

Put Together

EMC 3070
© Evan-Moor Corp.

Put Together

EMC 3070
© Evan-Moor Corp.

Put Together

EMC 3070
© Evan-Moor Corp.

Put Together

EMC 3070
© Evan-Moor Corp.

5	5	6	6
7	7	8	8
9	9	10	10

Put Together

EMC 3070
© Evan-Moor Corp.

Put Together

EMC 3070
© Evan-Moor Corp.

Put Together

EMC 3070
© Evan-Moor Corp.

Put Together

EMC 3070
© Evan-Moor Corp.

Put Together

EMC 3070
© Evan-Moor Corp.

Put Together

EMC 3070
© Evan-Moor Corp.

Put Together

EMC 3070
© Evan-Moor Corp.

Put Together

EMC 3070
© Evan-Moor Corp.

Put Together

EMC 3070
© Evan-Moor Corp.

Put Together

EMC 3070
© Evan-Moor Corp.

Put Together

EMC 3070
© Evan-Moor Corp.

Put Together

EMC 3070
© Evan-Moor Corp.

Take Away

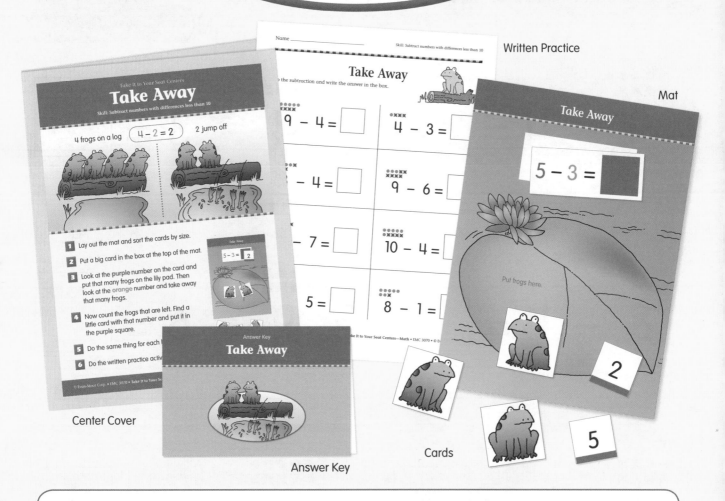

Center Cover

Written Practice

Mat

Cards

Answer Key

Skill: Subtract numbers with differences less than 10

Steps to Follow

1. **Prepare the center.** (See page 3.)

2. **Introduce the center.** State the goal. Say: *You will count and take away frogs to help you subtract one number from another number.*

3. **Teach the skill.** Demonstrate how to use the center with individual students or small groups.

4. **Practice the skill.** Have students use the center independently or with a partner.

Contents

Take Away

Do the subtraction and write the answer in the box.

9 – 4 =

4 – 3 =

8 – 4 =

9 – 6 =

9 – 7 =

10 – 4 =

5 – 5 =

8 – 1 =

Take Away

Skill: Subtract numbers with differences less than 10

4 frogs on a log $4 - 2 = 2$ 2 jump off

1. Lay out the mat and sort the cards by size.

2. Put a big card in the box at the top of the mat.

3. Look at the **purple** number on the card and put that many frogs on the lily pad. Then look at the **orange** number and take away that many frogs.

4. Now count the frogs that are left. Find a little card with that number and put it in the purple square.

5. Do the same thing for each big card.

6. Do the written practice activity.

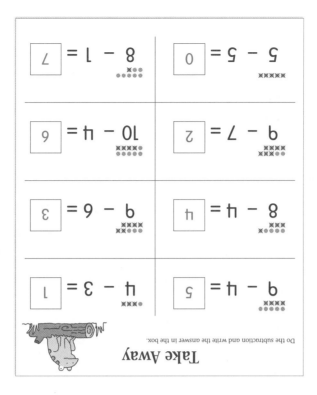

Take Away

Do the subtraction and write the answer in the box.

5 − 5 = [0]	8 − 1 = [7]
9 − 7 = [2]	10 − 4 = [6]
8 − 4 = [4]	9 − 6 = [3]
9 − 4 = [5]	4 − 3 = [1]

Written Practice

(fold)

Answer Key

Take Away

Take Away

$6 - 1 = 5$	$5 - 3 = 2$
$10 - 6 = 4$	$4 - 1 = 3$
$7 - 4 = 3$	$6 - 6 = 0$
$9 - 5 = 4$	$9 - 3 = 6$
$7 - 2 = 5$	$8 - 7 = 1$
$8 - 2 = 6$	$9 - 2 = 7$

Take Away

Put big card here.

Put frogs here.

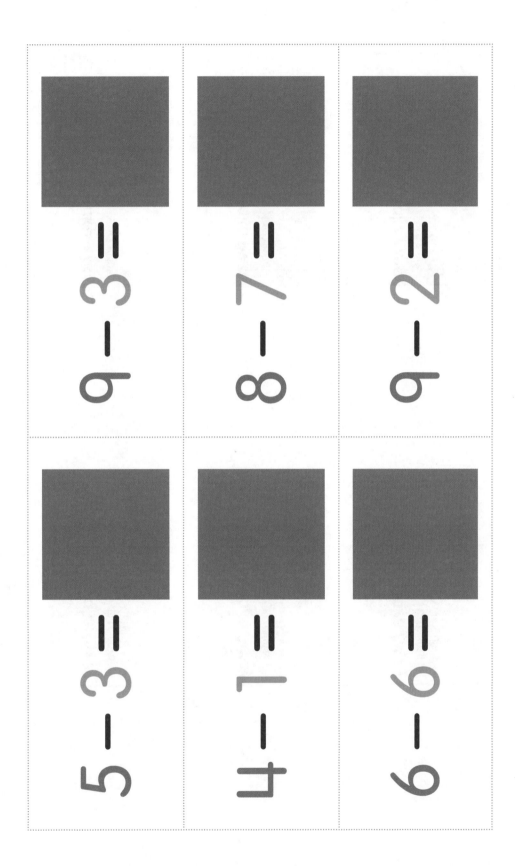

9 − 3 =

8 − 7 =

9 − 2 =

5 − 3 =

4 − 1 =

6 − 6 =

Take Away

EMC 3070
© Evan-Moor Corp.

Take Away

EMC 3070
© Evan-Moor Corp.

Take Away

EMC 3070
© Evan-Moor Corp.

Take Away

EMC 3070
© Evan-Moor Corp.

Take Away

EMC 3070
© Evan-Moor Corp.

Take Away

EMC 3070
© Evan-Moor Corp.

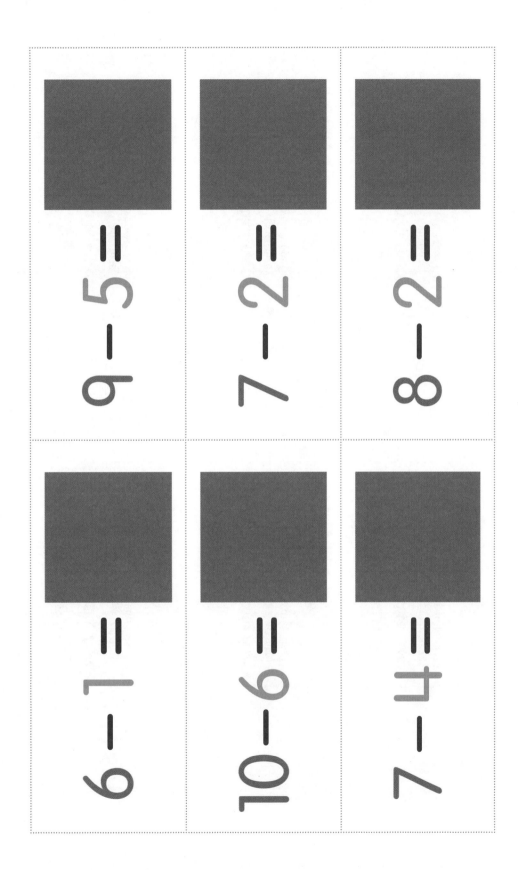

9 – 5 =

7 – 2 =

8 – 2 =

6 – 1 =

10 – 6 =

7 – 4 =

Take Away

EMC 3070
© Evan-Moor Corp.

Take Away

EMC 3070
© Evan-Moor Corp.

Take Away

EMC 3070
© Evan-Moor Corp.

Take Away

EMC 3070
© Evan-Moor Corp.

Take Away

EMC 3070
© Evan-Moor Corp.

Take Away

EMC 3070
© Evan-Moor Corp.

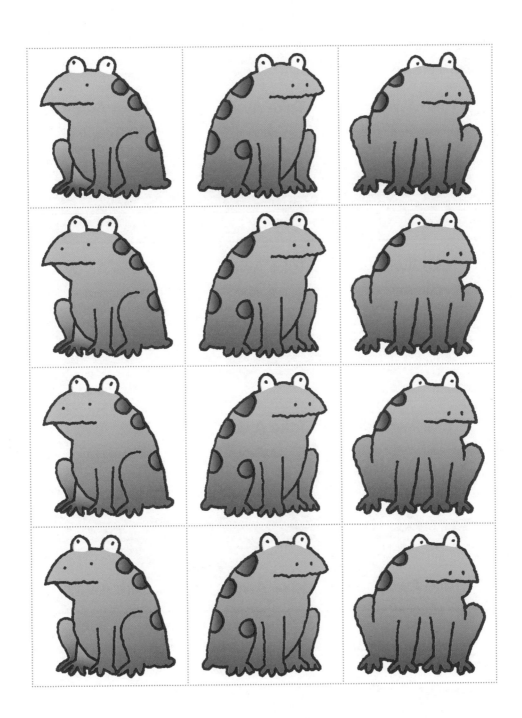

Take Away

EMC 3070
© Evan-Moor Corp.

Take Away

EMC 3070
© Evan-Moor Corp.

Take Away

EMC 3070
© Evan-Moor Corp.

Take Away

EMC 3070
© Evan-Moor Corp.

Take Away

EMC 3070
© Evan-Moor Corp.

Take Away

EMC 3070
© Evan-Moor Corp.

Take Away

EMC 3070
© Evan-Moor Corp.

Take Away

EMC 3070
© Evan-Moor Corp.

Take Away

EMC 3070
© Evan-Moor Corp.

Take Away

EMC 3070
© Evan-Moor Corp.

Take Away

EMC 3070
© Evan-Moor Corp.

Take Away

EMC 3070
© Evan-Moor Corp.

0	1	2	3
3	4	4	5
5	6	6	7

Take Away

EMC 3070
© Evan-Moor Corp.

Take Away

EMC 3070
© Evan-Moor Corp.

Take Away

EMC 3070
© Evan-Moor Corp.

Take Away

EMC 3070
© Evan-Moor Corp.

Take Away

EMC 3070
© Evan-Moor Corp.

Take Away

EMC 3070
© Evan-Moor Corp.

Take Away

EMC 3070
© Evan-Moor Corp.

Take Away

EMC 3070
© Evan-Moor Corp.

Take Away

EMC 3070
© Evan-Moor Corp.

Take Away

EMC 3070
© Evan-Moor Corp.

Take Away

EMC 3070
© Evan-Moor Corp.

Take Away

EMC 3070
© Evan-Moor Corp.

Add or Subtract

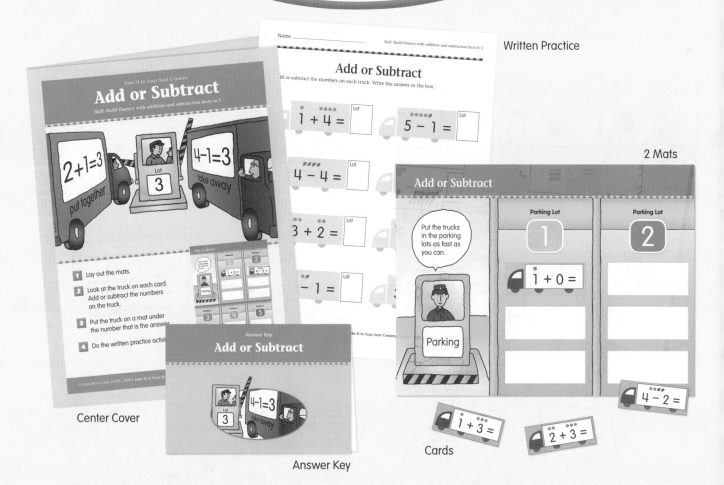

Center Cover

Answer Key

Written Practice

2 Mats

Cards

Skill: Build fluency with addition and subtraction facts to 5

Steps to Follow

1. **Prepare the center.** (See page 3.)

2. **Introduce the center.** State the goal. Say: *You will add or subtract the numbers on each card and then park the truck on a mat under the number that is the answer.*

3. **Teach the skill.** Demonstrate how to use the center with individual students or small groups.

4. **Practice the skill.** Have students use the center independently or with a partner.

Contents

Add or Subtract

Add or subtract the numbers on each truck. Write the answer in the box.

$1 + 4 =$ Lot

$5 - 1 =$ Lot

$4 - 4 =$ Lot

$2 + 1 =$ Lot

$3 + 2 =$ Lot

$3 + 1 =$ Lot

$2 - 1 =$ Lot

$3 - 1 =$ Lot

Add or Subtract

Skill: Build fluency with addition and subtraction facts to 5

1. Lay out the mats.

2. Look at the truck on each card. Add or subtract the numbers on the truck.

3. Put the truck on a mat under the number that is the answer.

4. Do the written practice activity.

Written Practice

Add or Subtract

Add or subtract the numbers on each truck. Write the answer in the box.

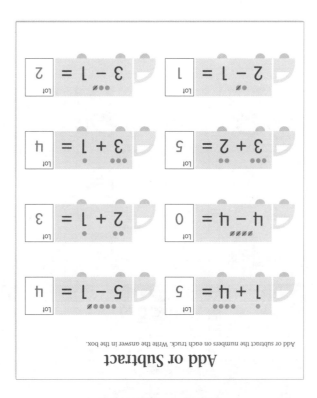

1 + 4 = 5	5 − 1 = 4
4 − 4 = 0	2 + 1 = 3
3 + 2 = 5	3 + 1 = 4
2 − 1 = 1	3 − 1 = 2

(fold)

Answer Key

Add or Subtract

Add or Subtract

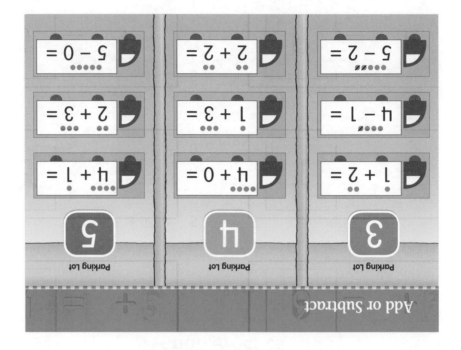

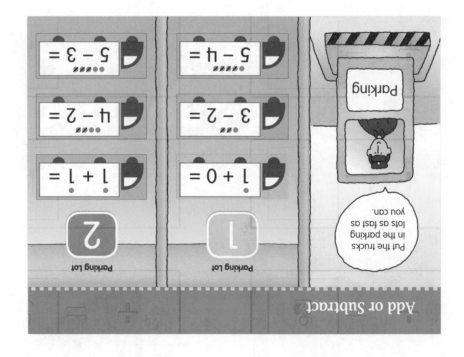

Add or Subtract

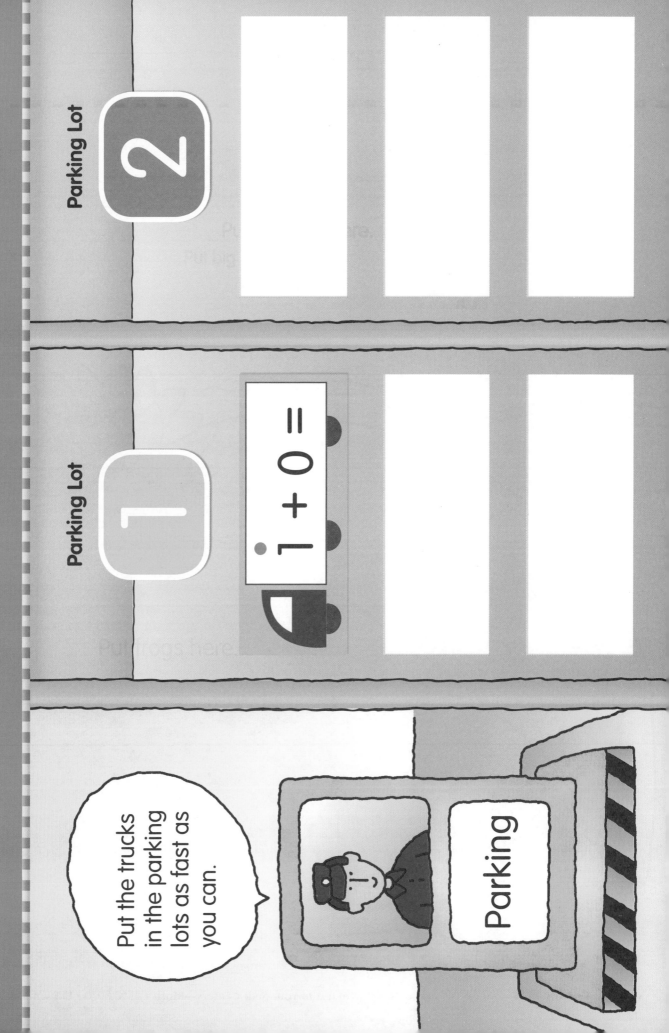

Parking Lot

2

Parking Lot

1

$1 + 0 =$

Put the trucks in the parking lots as fast as you can.

Parking

Add or Subtract

Parking Lot 5

Parking Lot 4

Parking Lot 3

3 − 2 =	4 + 1 =
5 − 4 =	4 + 0 =
1 + 1 =	1 + 3 =
4 − 2 =	2 + 2 =
5 − 3 =	2 + 3 =
5 − 2 =	4 − 1 =
1 + 2 =	5 − 0 =

Add or Subtract

EMC 3070
© Evan-Moor Corp.

Add or Subtract

EMC 3070
© Evan-Moor Corp.

Add or Subtract

EMC 3070
© Evan-Moor Corp.

Add or Subtract

EMC 3070
© Evan-Moor Corp.

Add or Subtract

EMC 3070
© Evan-Moor Corp.

Add or Subtract

EMC 3070
© Evan-Moor Corp.

Add or Subtract

EMC 3070
© Evan-Moor Corp.

Add or Subtract

EMC 3070
© Evan-Moor Corp.

Add or Subtract

EMC 3070
© Evan-Moor Corp.

Add or Subtract

EMC 3070
© Evan-Moor Corp.

Add or Subtract

EMC 3070
© Evan-Moor Corp.

Add or Subtract

EMC 3070
© Evan-Moor Corp.

Add or Subtract

EMC 3070
© Evan-Moor Corp.

Add or Subtract

EMC 3070
© Evan-Moor Corp.

My Clock

Written Practice

Mat

Center Cover

Answer Key

Cards

Skill: Know the parts of a clock

Steps to Follow

1. **Prepare the center.** (See page 3.)

2. **Introduce the center.** State the goal. Say: *You will move the hands on the big clock to match the time shown on each little clock.*

3. **Teach the skill.** Demonstrate how to use the center with individual students or small groups.

4. **Practice the skill.** Have students use the center independently or with a partner.

Contents

My Clock

Write the numbers on the clock.

What time is it?

My Clock

Skill: Know the parts of a clock

I have 2 hands.

1. Lay out the big clock.

2. Take a card with a little clock and look at the hands.

3. Move the hands on the big clock to match the little clock. Can you tell what time it is?

4. Do the same thing with each of the other little clocks.

5. Do the written practice activity.

What time is it? `3 : 0 0`

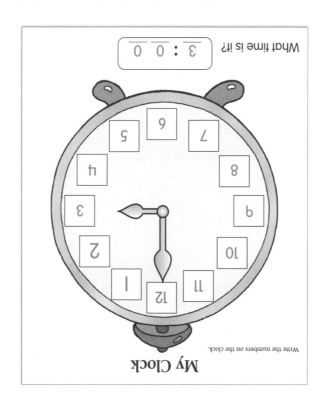

My Clock

Write the numbers on the clock.

Written Practice

(fold)

My Clock

My Clock

To the teacher:

This center emphasizes the placement of numbers on the face of a clock and the position of the clock's hands to show time by the hour.

The student will manipulate the moveable hands on the big clock to duplicate the time shown on each small clock. As a student works with this center, do a quick check to see that he or she has achieved the learning goal.

My Clock

Laminate the clock hands.
Attach them to the clock
with a brass paper fastener.

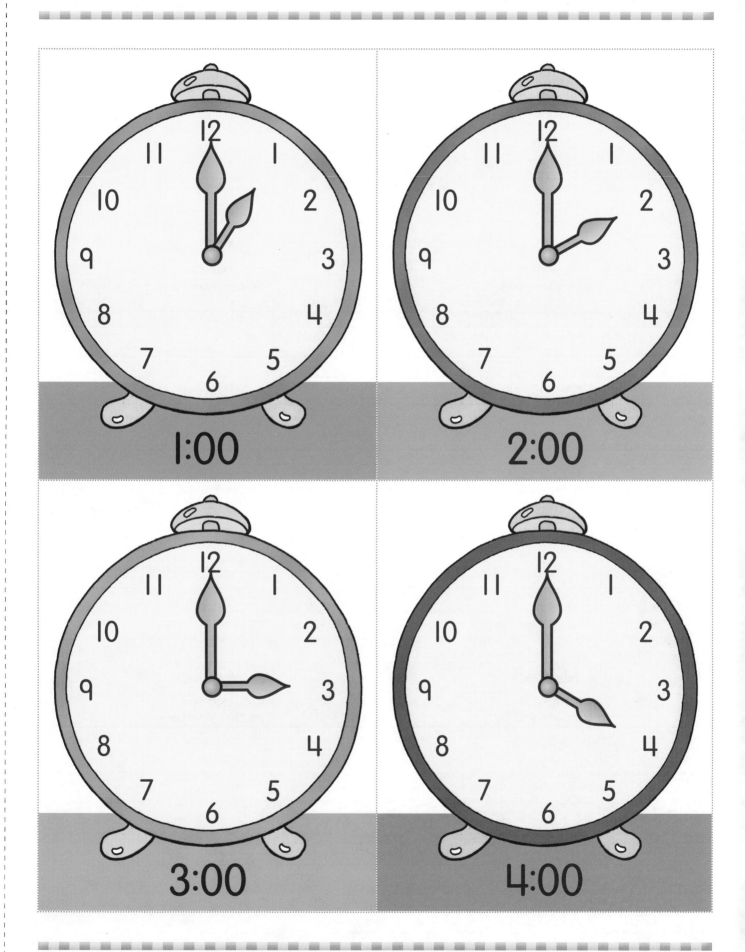

1:00

2:00

3:00

4:00

My Clock

EMC 3070
© Evan-Moor Corp.

My Clock

EMC 3070
© Evan-Moor Corp.

My Clock

EMC 3070
© Evan-Moor Corp.

My Clock

EMC 3070
© Evan-Moor Corp.

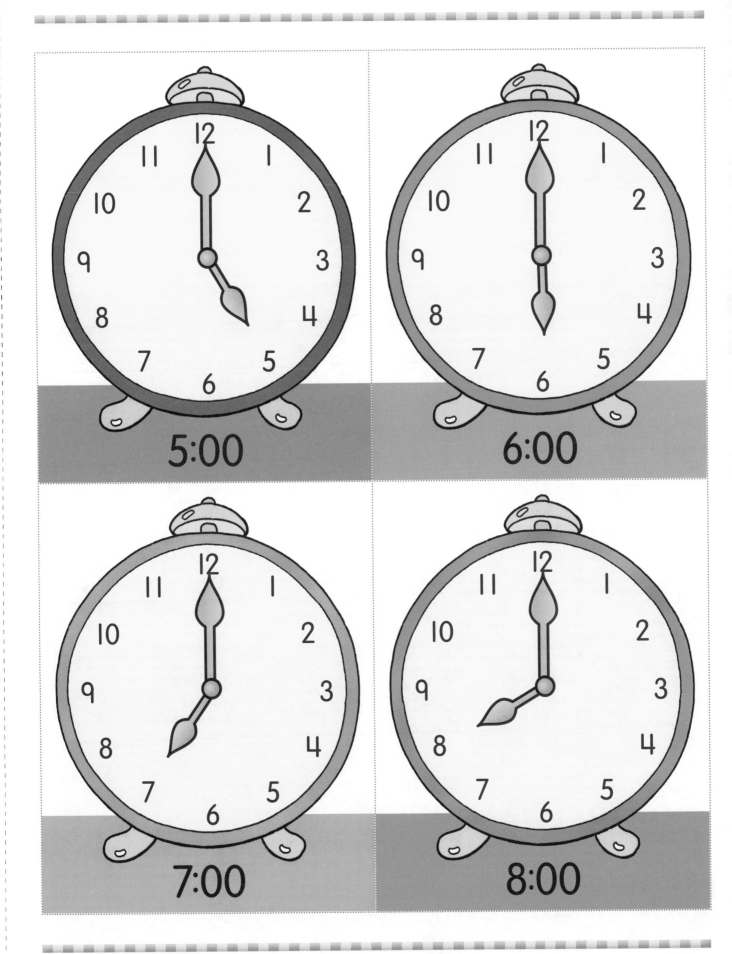

5:00

6:00

7:00

8:00

My Clock

EMC 3070
© Evan-Moor Corp.

My Clock

EMC 3070
© Evan-Moor Corp.

My Clock

EMC 3070
© Evan-Moor Corp.

My Clock

EMC 3070
© Evan-Moor Corp.

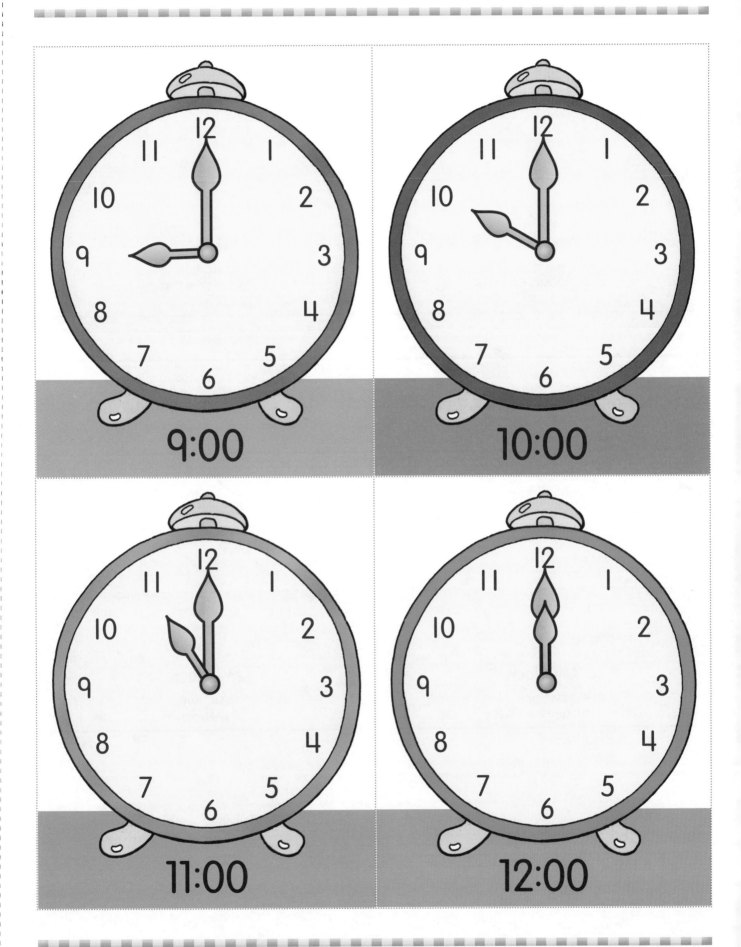

My Clock

EMC 3070
© Evan-Moor Corp.

My Clock

EMC 3070
© Evan-Moor Corp.

My Clock

EMC 3070
© Evan-Moor Corp.

My Clock

EMC 3070
© Evan-Moor Corp.

Shorter or Longer?

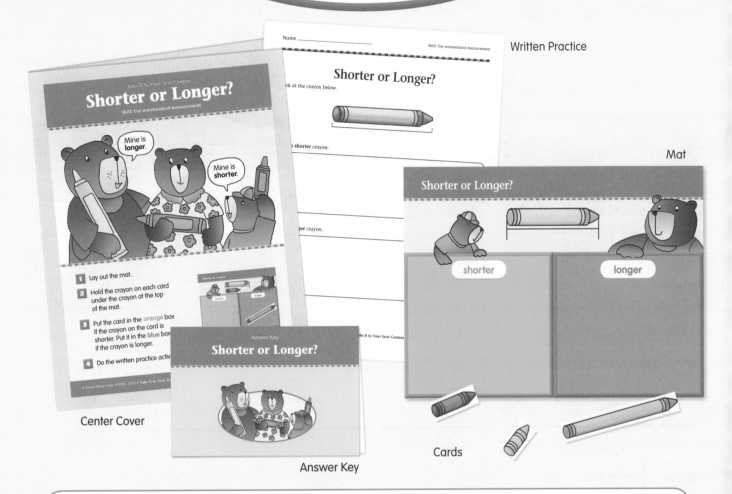

Written Practice

Mat

Center Cover

Answer Key

Cards

Skill: Use nonstandard measurement and comparative language

Steps to Follow

1. **Prepare the center.** (See page 3.)

2. **Introduce the center.** State the goal. Say: *You will compare the crayon on each card to the crayon on the mat and tell whether it is shorter or longer.*

3. **Teach the skill.** Demonstrate how to use the center with individual students or small groups.

4. **Practice the skill.** Have students use the center independently or with a partner.

Contents

Shorter or Longer?

Look at the crayon below.

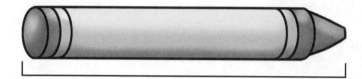

Draw a **shorter** crayon.

Draw a **longer** crayon.

Shorter or Longer?

Skill: Use nonstandard measurement

1 Lay out the mat.

2 Hold the crayon on each card under the crayon at the top of the mat.

3 Put the card in the orange box if the crayon on the card is shorter. Put it in the blue box if the crayon is longer.

4 Do the written practice activity.

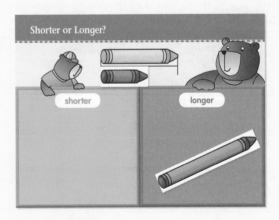

142 Take It to Your Seat Centers—Math • EMC 3070 • © Evan-Moor Corp.

Shorter or Longer?

Answer Key

(fold)

Written Practice

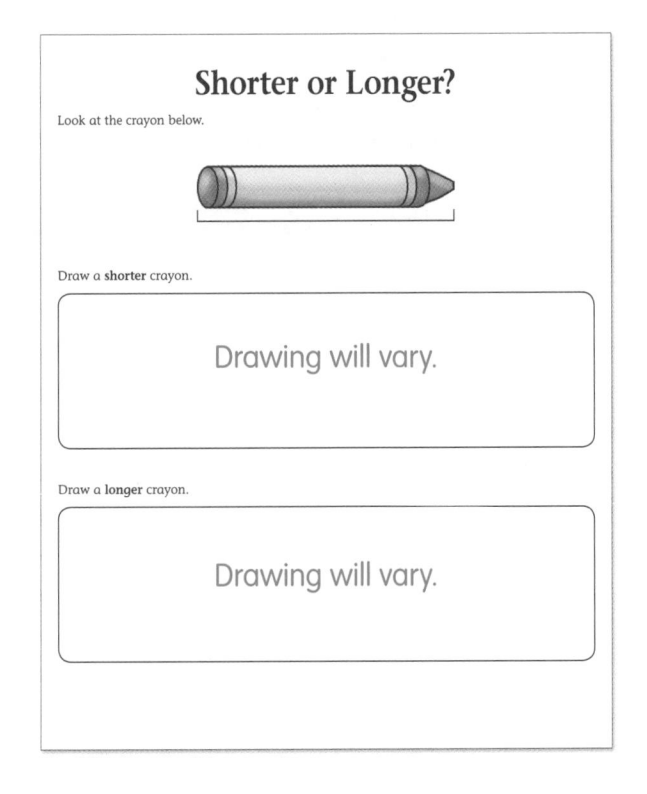

Shorter or Longer?

Look at the crayon below.

Draw a **shorter** crayon.

Drawing will vary.

Draw a **longer** crayon.

Drawing will vary.

Shorter or Longer?

Shorter or Longer?

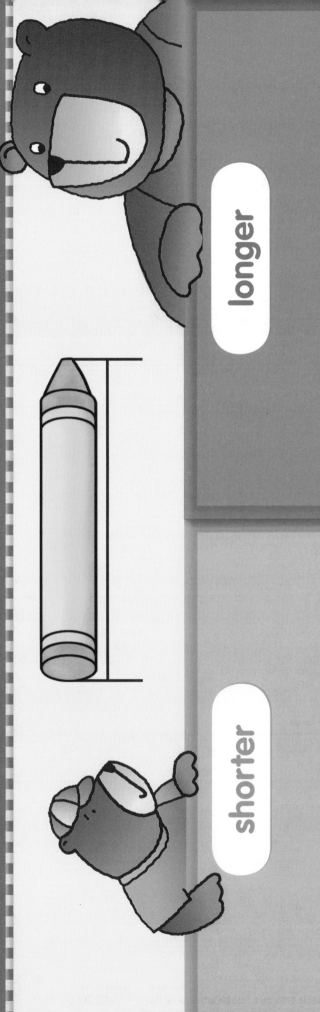

longer

shorter

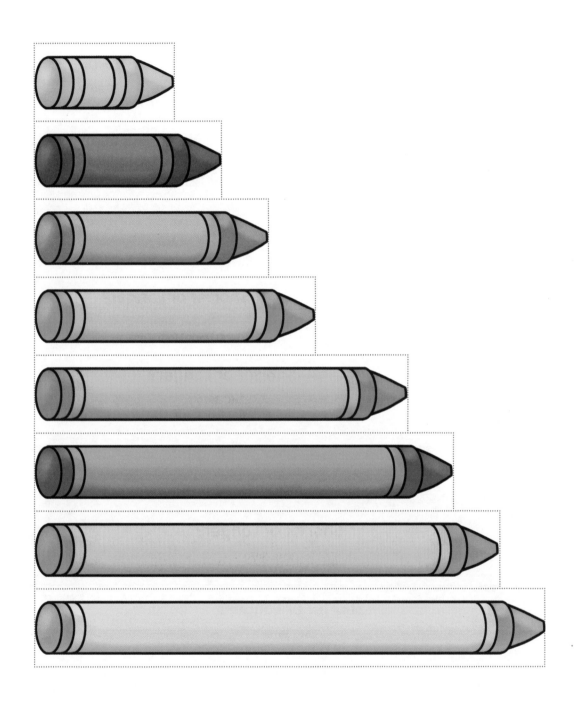

Shorter or Longer?

EMC 3070
© Evan-Moor Corp.

Shorter or Longer?

EMC 3070
© Evan-Moor Corp.

Shorter or Longer?

EMC 3070
© Evan-Moor Corp.

Shorter or Longer?

EMC 3070
© Evan-Moor Corp.

Shorter or Longer?

EMC 3070
© Evan-Moor Corp.

Shorter or Longer?

EMC 3070
© Evan-Moor Corp.

Shorter or Longer?

EMC 3070
© Evan-Moor Corp.

Shorter or Longer?

EMC 3070
© Evan-Moor Corp.

Sort Shapes

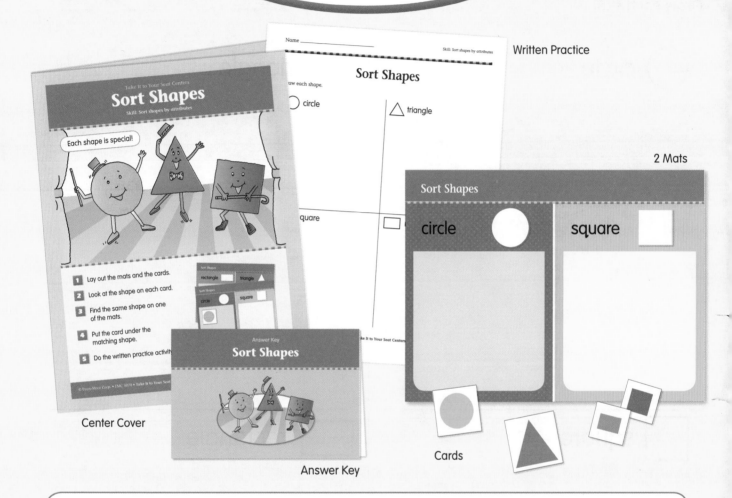

Written Practice

2 Mats

Center Cover

Answer Key

Cards

Skill: Sort shapes by attributes

Steps to Follow

1. **Prepare the center.** (See page 3.)

2. **Introduce the center.** State the goal. Say: *You will match the shape on each card to a shape on the mats.*

3. **Teach the skill.** Demonstrate how to use the center with individual students or small groups.

4. **Practice the skill.** Have students use the center independently or with a partner.

Contents

Sort Shapes

Draw each shape.

 circle

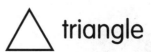 triangle

square

rectangle

Sort Shapes

Skill: Sort shapes by attributes

Each shape is special!

1 Lay out the mats and the cards.

2 Look at the shape on each card.

3 Find the same shape on one of the mats.

4 Put the card under the matching shape.

5 Do the written practice activity.

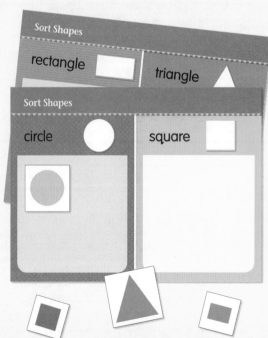

Written Practice

Sort Shapes

Draw each shape.

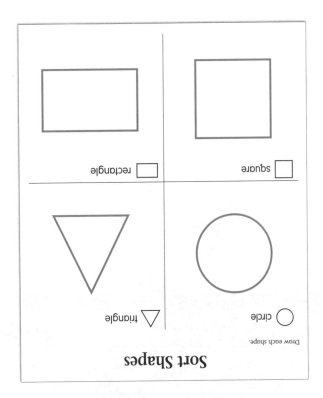

circle ◯

triangle △

square □

rectangle ▭

(fold)

Answer Key

Sort Shapes

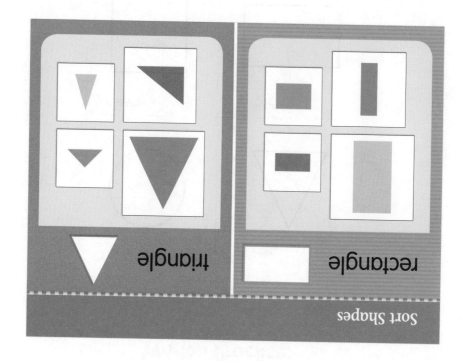

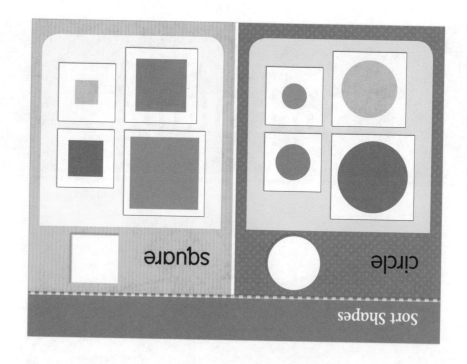

Sort Shapes

EMC 3070
© Evan-Moor Corp.

Sort Shapes

EMC 3070
© Evan-Moor Corp.

Sort Shapes

EMC 3070
© Evan-Moor Corp.

Sort Shapes

EMC 3070
© Evan-Moor Corp.

Sort Shapes

EMC 3070
© Evan-Moor Corp.

Sort Shapes

EMC 3070
© Evan-Moor Corp.

Sort Shapes

EMC 3070
© Evan-Moor Corp.

Sort Shapes

EMC 3070
© Evan-Moor Corp.

Sort Shapes

EMC 3070
© Evan-Moor Corp.

Sort Shapes

EMC 3070
© Evan-Moor Corp.

Sort Shapes

EMC 3070
© Evan-Moor Corp.

Sort Shapes

EMC 3070
© Evan-Moor Corp.

Sort Shapes

EMC 3070
© Evan-Moor Corp.

Sort Shapes

EMC 3070
© Evan-Moor Corp.

Sort Shapes

EMC 3070
© Evan-Moor Corp.

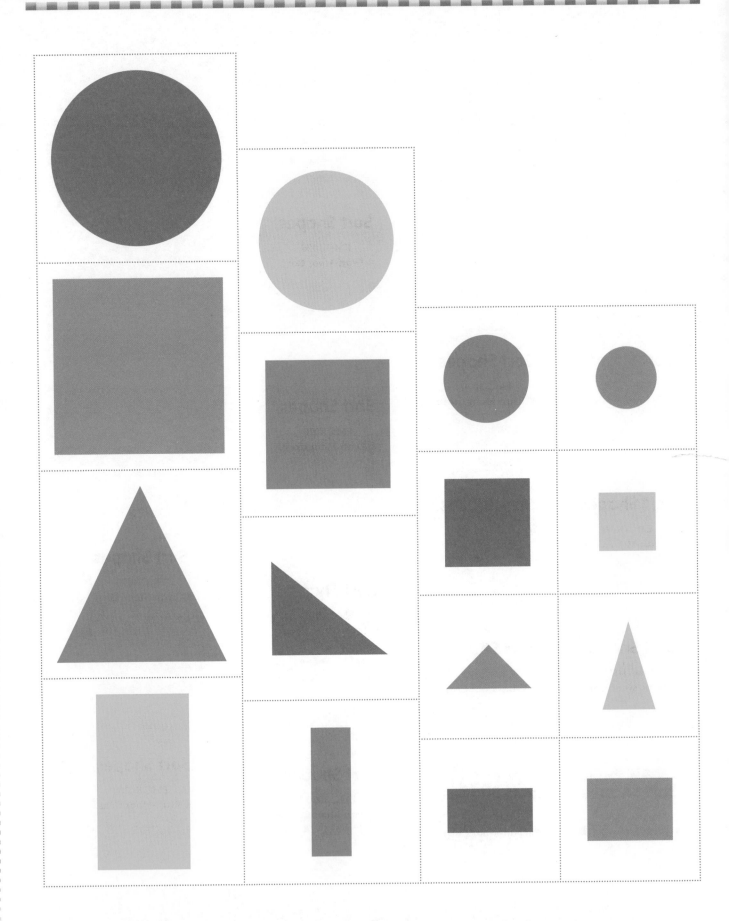

Sort Shapes

triangle

rectangle

Sort Shapes

square

circle